SUGA

Caribbean Short Stories and Poems

from St. Kitts and Nevis

For Pastor & Sis Laurence Brown.
I hope you enjoy this
little "visit" to St. Kitts
and Nevis.

Sincerely,
Annette Michael
8/2/01

by

Annette Walwyn Michael

Sugar Is All
Copyright © 2001
Annette Walwyn Michael

Sugar Is All is a collection of fictitious short stories and poems.
Though the author uses some family names and references to
familiar places in St. Kitts and Nevis, the work is imaginative.
Resemblance to any person alive or dead is purely coincidental.

Library of Congress Control Number: 2001126455
ISBN: 0-9660456-8-8

Printed in the United States by:
Morris Publishing
3212 East Highway 30
Kearney, NE 68847
1-800-650-7888
Fax: 1-308-237-0263
http://morrispublishing.com
email:publish@morrispublishing.com

Dedication

To Reg, Sharon, Egypt June, and Marlene

Acknowledgments

The author would like to make the following acknowledgments:

To Our Heavenly Father, for His Gifts—especially those of creativity and memory.

To Mrs. Helen Mclean of St. Kitts, my English teacher, for countless years of inspiration. You showed me that words live and breathe, and that I should respect and appreciate them. You gave me, as a child, the "gift of story."

To Mrs. Jean D'Costa, my English Professor and mentor. You introduced me to an appreciation for Caribbean literature. Then you gave me helpful feedback when I began my own writing.

To the 1992 National Humanities class in the Research Triangle Park, North Carolina, and Richard Schramm, director. Those three weeks in the summer of 1992 inspired me to write my own short stories.

To Aunt Katy (Taylor) and Aunt Mae (Wayner) for reading the entire volume and giving me my first Kittitian/Nevisian critical guidance. I needed every word of your feedback

To all of my students at Northeastern Academy, Uniondale High School, Far Rockaway High School, and York College. You "tried my stories on for size" and assured me that they "fit."

To my colleagues at Far Rockaway High School who found the time to read and critique a story or two, and who helped with manuscript preparation. You really encouraged me.

To Reginald McKnight and my class at the Chenango Valley Writers' Conference in 1997. I learned so much from each of you.

To my sister and brother-in-law, Amorelle and Eno, both successful writers. You gave me the courage to follow the example you set.

And to my husband, Reg, and my daughters, Sharon, Egypt June, and Marlene. You provided the time, space, and support I needed to create these stories and poems.

Many, many thanks.

Table of Contents

Scrapbook

1.

Sugar Is All

The loud blast of the factory horn awakened Nathan Carty from a peaceful sleep. He awoke quickly, stretched, and opened the louver windows to let out the stale night air. Standing at the window he inhaled the fresh air deeply. Life was good. Twenty years at the sugar factory had seen Nathan rise from handler to foreman. Twenty good years, he thought. Walking around the house in Irish Town, Nathan admired the new settee that he recently ordered from Puerto Rico. The spotless kitchen floor was covered with new, oily-smelling linoleum. A stainless-steel sink was installed just three months before, replacing the chipped enamel sink that was more than ten years old.

Yes, Nathan sighed. The factory work was good for him. He boasted to his friends that his wife Lilli never had to work. Nathan had married her from her father's house and had given her everything she needed and more than what most of her neighbors would ever own. That sugar-cane factory had been the "godfather" of his family for years, feeding and clothing his grandfather, his father, and now himself. "Sugar is all" was a family maxim, accounting for the stylish dresses from the Virgin Islands, to new shoes from St. Martin, and to cupboards stacked with food.

Sugar even gave some bonuses. Often Nathan would bring home the sweet Muscovado sugar, the dark heavy molasses, or bottles of fresh cane juice—all from different stages of the sugar processing. As foreman, this was one privilege that he enjoyed. And to think it did not have to end. By the time he was ready to retire at 55, young Natty, now in Form Four at the Grammar School, would be able to start working at the factory. Nathan had it all figured out.

If only he could persuade Natty to love the factory as his father did. Just the day before, when Nathan brought home his paycheck to his wife, joking, "Look what you godfather send this

3

week," Natty had sucked his teeth as quietly as he could. That same day, when Natty's Grammar School class had a field trip to the factory to see the process of making sugar, Natty had such a stomach ache that he had to stay home for the day. The stomachache disappeared about four o'clock, though, and Natty was able to go to football practice at Warner Park. That Thursday evening, as Nathan Carty peeled a stalk of soft sugar cane before supper, he confronted his son:

"I see all the boys in you class at the factory today, all 'cept you. Wha happen, Natty-boy?"

Young Nathan winced. He hated to be called Natty, Nate, or worse yet, Natty-boy. At school his teachers called him Nathan, or Carty. His friends called him Nat. Why couldn't his parents grow up? "Natty-Boy" was all right when he was five, but now?

"I'm too old for that name, now, Dad, and besides, you can't call me that when I'm working as a civil servant in some office in Basseterre," the boy joked.

"I will call you what ever I feel like, you hear? Is only one man in this house, and two man crab can't live in one hole. And I still want to know what happen to you today. You sick sick and can't go to school, but you well enough to go kill yourself on the football field. Furthermore, what is this you talking about— going to work as a civil servant? I tell you already, sugar is all, Man. Sugar put pap in you mouth from the time you born. Sugar put nice pants and shirt to cover you body and a house for you to sleep in. Is sugar give you strength to talk foolishness 'bout how you want to be a civil servant. You ain't have no ambition?"

"Yes, I have great plans, Dad." Natty moved closer to his father. This subject, his future, was one he loved to talk about.

"I want to get at least seven subjects at O-level, then do the A-level. After that I want to go to the University and get..."

"Is what foolishness I hearing in me house? You ain't no scholar. What university you talking 'bout? I training you for the factory. Sugar feed me father, me grandfather, and me. And sugar going feed you, too. Don't let me hear no more of this stupidness, you hear?"

Nathan moved to the window for relief from the anger that made him tremble. He wanted to hold that child and slap some sense into him. This was not the first time Natty had shown his disgust for his father's job, but Nathan had tried to ignore the signs of rebellion. Perhaps if he just waited a while, the boy would see things his father's way. He wanted his son to get a good education. That is why he had sent him to the prestigious Grammar School. With some O-level subjects under his belt, he could become a foreman earlier than his father did. He may not even have to start as a lowly handler, loading the cane into the cleaning bins as his father had. It was hard, messy, work, but it was a start. Perhaps one day, Nathan hoped, his son could be the Factory Manager. His son. But now, at fifteen years of age, when he should already be mastering the machete in the cane field, here he was talking foolishness. Nathan's trembling fingers tried to open the louvers, but they were already open. Without thinking, he kept turning the handle until he felt it give way in his hand. Throwing the broken handle to the floor in disgust, he dropped to the settee, his face in his hands. Why? Why? Why? Nathan felt that if he did not scream something inside him would burst like an overripe soursop.

At the open window, Nathan Carty looked toward the lights of the factory in the distance. A long, loud blast was calling the evening shift to work. He listened, and he remembered... Nathan recalled looking forward to trips to the factory with his own father—the long ride on his father's bicycle, the sweet, sticky smell of crushed cane stalks, the sound of boiling liquid, the slowly-moving, thick Muscovado sugar. Nathan Carty could never forget his first taste of molasses, straight from the churning bin, or the sight of mountains of warm brown sugar ready for shipping. Nathan Carty thought of the days when, aching for another chance to visit the factory with his father, he had to settle for less—fixing his father's lunch in the steel heating pans, and putting the pans near the door for his father to pick them up on his way out. Even as a boy, Nathan could think of one thing:

"One of these days...One of these days...."

And now, this ungrateful child, this fool that he had for a son, talking about "Civil Servant" and "University." The words were like bitter bush in his mouth and in his belly. Nathan refused his supper of roasted breadfruit and steamed potfish that night and went to bed early.

The factory horn awakened Nathan as usual the next day, Friday morning. He had tossed most of the night and had fallen into a deep sleep at foreday morning. The cocks had stopped crowing, and the mosquitoes had retired, but the chickens were loudly scratching for worms in the yard. Nathan's bowl of hot cornmeal porridge with cinnamon leaf was ready, but he was not hungry. He ate two hot johnny cakes and drank his vervine bush tea. Carefully avoiding his son, Nathan left for work as soon as he could.

At the factory, Nathan checked his clipboard. Yes, his crew had arrived. His shift worked the front end this week, loading the cleaning bins with piles of freshly cut cane. When the men were assigned their duties, Nathan had time to think. He knew that his wife Lilli was suffering. That morning she had complained of pains in her stomach. She, the woman who never murmured, even when her womb appeared to be sealed. Nathan knew she needed to deal with the stress doing strange things to every organ in her body. Last night as he embraced her he seemed to be holding a statue. She lay stiff, awake, silent. Nathan knew that like him, she was thinking back...

"You cannot have children," the doctor had said when, swallowing his pride, Nathan had allowed his wife to drag him to Doctor Lake's office down by the Square. After six years of marriage no offspring had come. Refusing to accept the verdict of childlessness, Nathan brought home sea moss, boiled it himself, and added condensed milk. That remedy was supposed to be a sure recipe for procreation. Nothing happened. Then he tried sassparilla, boiling the bush even stronger than suggested. Nathan drank the tea every day and night for a month. He even washed himself with the leaves, taking the strong smell to his job with him. His wife's menses still came with annoying regularity. Friends recommended the obeah man, but Nathan declined that offer. He was not going to stoop so low. As the seventh anniversary of his marriage to Lilli was approaching, Nathan began to contemplate the obeah suggestion, when the miracle happened.

The child was conceived without any help from herb or hedonics. The beautiful, brown, miracle baby was born on a bright Thursday morning. Nathan's child, Natty, the one that both opened and sealed up the womb. For Lilli bore no more children after Natty.

Nathan Carty had celebrated the birth of that child for weeks. There had been lots of souse, black pudding, goat water, rice and pigeon peas. Empty cases of Vita malt and beer had piled up high outside the house in Irish Town. Nathan couldn't believe that he finally had a child, a boy child, at last... someone to take his place at the factory one day. Now he wondered, was this some sort of Trojan gift like the one Nathan had read about in primary school—the one that would unload a bellyful of problems?

That evening, Nathan noticed that young Natty seemed to be studying his books with a passion, as if he was studying for spite. The boy casually left some papers where his parents could see them. His marks were good and one teacher had commented, "Work shows considerable promise." Sticking out of his *History of the British Commonwealth* was an application form for the University of Miami. His father saw it and his fried goatfish almost choked him. Nathan noted that his wife glanced at the application and then began humming quietly. Almost inaudibly, ignoring the presence of the child, Lilli suggested to her husband,

"Perhaps you should ask someone to speak to him...perhaps his Godmother."

"What stupidness you talking 'bout, woman? De fool ain't want to have nothing to do with he own Godfather that feed and clothe him and put a roof over his head. But I telling you: Who don't hear will feel. Mark my words: Who don't hear will feel."

Next morning, the factory horn had a strange sound—a long low, mournful blast. It blew ten minutes before the normal time, so Nathan hurried out to work, in his haste forgetting his lunch pan. He pedaled his bicycle to the factory, joined by other anxious-looking workers. No one seemed able to explain the change in the factory's blast. Was a hurricane coming? Was the crop finishing early? Had someone "big" died? Speculations flew, but no one could give a solid answer.

The factory was quiet that morning. Usually, bedroom and bathroom jokes abounded as the men worked the machines, but Nathan noticed that today an awful stillness hung over the place interrupted now and then by hurried steps of the men who usually worked in the main office. In their white shirts and ties, the "Bossmen," as they were called, looked out-of-place in the misty-sweet, noisy rooms. They spoke to no one, but hurriedly checked the heaters, the clarifiers, the filters—machines they were not accustomed to checking. The loud sugar evaporators muffled but could not quite hide their hurrying footsteps. Worried by a faceless, unnamed fear, Nathan worked his shift at the bagging station, where all morning his men stored the raw sugar into 50-pound bags for storage, and then he took his lunch break.

When he stepped outside in the warm sunshine, the midday factory blast was still blowing, again mournful, long, and loud. Near the red hibiscus bushes small groups of workmen had already assembled. Nathan's ears, accustomed to the usual clang of the steel pans, strained in vain to hear the men beginning to eat. What was going on? Why was no one eating? Nathan shaded his eyes as he adjusted to the light, and then as his vision cleared he noticed a young man in a school uniform standing apart in the shade of a flamboyant tree. Natty had brought his father's forgotten lunch pan and was listening to his portable radio. All awkwardness of the previous evening was forgotten as he rushed to his father, words spilling out of his mouth like water from a broken standpipe.

"Dad, I'm so sorry. I'm so sorry. I heard the news at school this morning. What you going to do?"

"What you talking 'bout, Natty? What happen? I ain't hear nothing. I just hungry, that's all, and now you bring me lunch. Thanks, Man."

"So you didn't hear? You ain't know? Listen. The midday news coming on now. I thought you did know."

As Nathan Carty listened to ZIZ, the local radio station, he heard this news:

"According to a release from the Associated Press, the price of sugar has dropped significantly on the world market. All levels of sugar production in St. Kitts and the rest of the Caribbean will have to cut back immediately to accommodate the new prices of sugar. Many jobs have been threatened. Most foremen will have to be laid off... This change has been caused in part by the success of the beet sugar industry in the United States and France——"

Feeling as if a whirlwind had occupied his head, Nathan Carty sat down on a bale of bagass and took the lunch pan from his son. Trembling fingers opened the lid mechanically, and the man looked at the conkee, the codfish, the sweet pumpkin as if they were foreign objects. Then he spoke at to his son:

"I know you got to go back to school. Thanks, Man. I glad you bring me lunch for me." He made no reference to his threatened job, the pink slip that could in an instant be the sinkhole to all his plans and dreams. However, as his son turned to pedal off on his own bicycle, he heard his father say:

"Study hard in school, you hear? Listen to your teachers. And when I come home tonight I think is time for us to look at that thing—the application form for the college. You still have it?"

2.

Wedding Chills

"Eh Eh, you hear wha me hear?"

Heads turned in the yard, but no one stopped working. Miss Ruthie's rhythmic grating of shelled coconut continued. She was making sugar cakes for the shop. Mannie continued cleaning jackfish in a far corner. Shaded by the Bombay mango tree, he was taking the guts from the scaled fish to the delight of a cloud of buzzing flies. Salome's squeak-squeak as she washed the clothes toned town slightly and she pushed her shoulder blades together to ease her aching back.

"All you no want to hear who going get married?"

Pride kept the yard sounds going. No one wanted to appear too nuff. But Miss Ruthie knew she had everyone's attention. A wedding in Basseterre was a holiday, a communal event. No matter where the wedding took place, at the Catholic Church by the Square or in the big Anglican Church on Cayon Street, there was always a crowd—not a crowd of guests, not those invited guests who had to wear their stiff can-can and crinoline. I am talking about everyone else who would leave the frying pan, the basin of dirty clothes, or the floor half scrubbed to "see de bride" and comment loudly about the merits or demerits of each guest.

Attending a wedding in Basseterre was like walking the gangplank. Dangerous insults, like well-aimed stones, struck guests from all directions. Often, guests had to be bribed to attend a wedding, and only the bravest or most brazen took the challenge.

"Well, me hear Dr. Lloyd son going get married."

"You mean that ramgoat?"

"De same one."

"Who so stupid to go marry he?"

"A hear is a girl from Anguilla."

"A where else Lloydie was going find a girl to marry he? Dem Anguilla girl an dem moo moo."

"Is only a stupid woman going marry dat ramscallion, some moomoo girl who don't know Lloydie."

"You sure Lloydie going show up for this wedding?"

" 'Member when he leave Miss Mable daughter in the church at Sandy Point, and the girl end up in the crazy house?"

"Yeah, and 'member when he up by the airport taking off in LIAT and Miss Moses daughter waiting for him at the Pilgrim Holiness Church?"

"Yeah, and 'member how Miss Moses husband sharpen he machete so long that night and just grinding he teeth waiting for Lloydie to come back?"

"Well, Me Dear, I ain't missing that wedding. Where you say it is? The Anglican Church? Thursday half-day, you say? A going bring me tray of sugar cake and tart. A know plenty people going buy. And Mannie, if jackfish running, bring some. You going find plenty people to buy you fish and them. Daddy-O, me can't wait till Thursday. Me can't wait."

In Royal bank the following Thursday morning, the young tellers worked briskly, constantly looking at their watches. Customers were in a hurry to have their business done, too. The question was often asked, "You going to the wedding?" The more affluent customers did not have to answer. Most already had brown paper curlers in their pressed hair. One customer had a ten o'clock appointment with the hairdresser.

Bank customers who had not been invited to the wedding were making their own plans so that they could get the best view of the wedding and the best gossip:

"A think de best place is by de fence. Then you can see everybody walking up to the church."

"No, man. Stand by the church door. Then if it rain, you just go inside. "

"For true, but I still prefer by the fence."

"You think Lloydie going come?"

"A hear the girl whole family coming from Anguilla. He better show up."

11

"A hear people coming from England—some Lord Somebody coming, for the girl father is a big man in the government."

"A hope the girl ain't going lose she mind. The crazy house done full enough of people Lloydie turn insane."

"You right, girl. We just got to wait and see."

Most of Basseterre was quiet that Thursday afternoon. As usual, the town had closed for half day. Even the boat to Nevis was not running. Women selling mangoes, bananas, and ground provisions down by the bay had gone home—no customers. Central Street, Victoria Road—no one in sight. But near Cayon Street, one could see the action. Market clothes, bank uniforms, factory workclothes—every attire was visible as the curious lined the church fence.

The organist, anticipating early arrivals, had begun to play calming music. Guests began to walk the mine field through the crowd. But today, there would be no heckling of guests. There were no catcalls to the young women or comments on how tight the men's clothes were. Everyone was looking, looking for that white car to pull up—the car with the groom.

A white Ford stopped impressively. The crowd hushed, hearts pounding. Then a groan:

"Is only the bride. Where that Lloydie? Don't tell me he going do the same thing again?"

"A hear the girl father have a gun."

"But what de use if he don't have anyone to use it on?"

"You think Lloydie going come?"

"Ask she."

The speaker pointed to his left where a disheveled young woman forced her way through the crowd. She mumbled to herself and dragged her worn slippers on the concrete walk:

"Lloydie, Lloydie, you know how a love you. You know how you love me, now and forever." Her demented chant drove shivers into the hearts of her hearers. She had been Lloydie's last victim.

"Look, British Airways jet taking off from the airport. I wonder if Lloydie on it going to England?"

"He can't go too far this time. The next place he going find is the jail. Is criminal what he doing, criminal. The judge aught to arrest him for breach of the law."

"What law?"

"Any law, man. That boy is a common criminal."

Then, like a flock of feeding pigeons, the crowd hushed again, for the bride's door opened. Accompanied by her father and attendants, she stepped toward the wrought-iron gates. There is something about a bride that silences a crowd. The most vulgar remark could be made about her guests, her attendants, even. But the bride commands respect. It is her day. Expressions of sympathy mixed with murmurs of admiration:

"Lloydie musta choose the prettiest girl in Anguilla."

"She dress musta cost the whose treasury. Look how the sequins shining in the sun. And watch the train! It long like the... Me ain't even know. Me never see a train so long, me dear."

"She smiling. You think she know what she doing?"

"Me dear child! She is one brave woman to wait for Lloydie in the church. I would stay right out here in that car till he show up."

The bride's procession moved through the hushed crowd to the door of the Anglican church. The organ music blared, and suddenly there was a great shout:

"He in the church already. Lloydie in the church."

"How he get in there and nobody see him? He must be a jumbie."

But Lloydie was no jumbie, no ghost. Outsmarting the busybodies, he had sneaked into the church hours early—to avoid changing his mind? To pray? To make a confession? Who knows? Nevertheless, Lloydie the heartbreaker, Lloydie the promise breaker had finally said, "I do." Lloydie emerged from the church as the organist played a recessional, his Anguillan bride at his side. But above the noise of the crowd a mad voice ranted:

"Lloydie, you know how I love you, now and forever..."

3.

Up Oxford Street

Mrs. Sexton had always looked old, even to her contemporaries. No one in Basseterre could remember her being called any other name than "Old Mrs. Sexton." As long as anyone in Basseterre could recall, she had always lived on Oxford Street and had always gone to the big Anglican Church on Seaton Street.

No one would see her during the week, but they would know she was alive because of the curtains that were opened at precisely 7:45 a.m. Students going to school would set their watches by it. And students going home late after netball or football practice could know the time by looking up at Mrs. Sexton's windows. The curtains closed at precisely 5:45 every day.

On Sunday Mrs. Sexton would emerge at 10:50 a.m. for her short walk to the Anglican Church. Dressed in her silk gloves and hat, she seemed the perfect English woman. Rumor had it that she had entertained the Queen privately and had served her scones and tea. No one had evidence to support the rumor but no one had evidence to the contrary either, so the story had become something of a legend. "Mrs. Sexton, the woman de Queen did go by," was as much a part of her name as the" Mrs." No one could remember her husband either, or whether or not she was ever really married.

Mrs. Sexton had gone to Miss Pickard's School up Oxford Street. Those were the "good old days" she would always say. Miss Pickard, a teacher from England, had obtained the former Governor's residence as a private school for girls. Of course, the school was for the gentlemen's daughters of Basseterre, to prepare them to be the ladies who lived in fancy homes up the Factory or up the Fort.

Miss Pickard's had rules, Mrs. Sexton would say. RULES. That is what had made a lady out of her. One rule stated that all girls must walk on the right side of the road only on their way to school. No Grammar School boys could go near Miss Pickard's precious charges. No, Sir. The boys going to Grammar School, up the same street, must walk on the left side of the road. This way the girls could remain ladies. LADIES.

Another rule was for the dress. The girls wore starched, white pinafores and white hats to school. White for Purity. Miss Pickard knew how to make LADIES. Yes, Sir. Ladies who knew their Latin and French and their Geometry theorems. Ladies who knew how to set a table for tea, and how to prepare scones. Ladies like Mrs. Sexton.

She sat at her window after those curtains were opened at 7:45 a.m. each day. Though the girls from Miss Pickard's School and the boys from Grammar School could not see her, she could see them, and as she sipped her morning tea, she sighed happily. Yes. Life was good, and the old traditions were strong. The girls still lit the lamp every day, and they still walked on the left side of the road. Miss Pickard's School was still making Ladies. Yes, Sir.

Mrs. Sexton knew that trouble was on the way, however, when she heard that Miss Pickard was going back to England. Her heart fluttered. As she put the scones into the oven, her hands trembled and her facial muscles tightened painfully. Her morning tea tasted bitter that day.

It was just not right. What was going to become of Basseterre? Things would never be the same again. No Sir. Not without Miss Pickard.

Mrs. Sexton watched anxiously and nervously, fully expecting the girls to become wild and barge down Oxford Street. She was sure that the girls would cut their hair and grow beards. As she looked, however, everything appeared the same. The girls still seemed like ladies. They still wore white school uniforms, and they still walked down the left side of the street.

One year passed. Two years. Mrs. Sexton had entertained the new principal, a petite English lady named Miss Langley. She was no Miss Pickard, but she would do.

A third September rolled around, and as Mrs. Sexton looked out of her window at 7:45 a.m. she fell back on her divan, fanning herself vigorously. When she caught her breath, and looked again, she closed her curtains quickly. No! She would not look out again. She couldn't. Had she really seen girls in *brown* pinafores and *cream* blouses? Did she really see *ties* at the girls necks?

Such things would never have happened if Miss Pickard had stayed in Basseterre. It was that Miss Langley, Mrs. Sexton said to herself. Miss Langley did not care that Basseterre needed ladies who knew how to dress, how to prepare scones, how to wear gloves. Ladies who knew how to wear white, not brown and cream like some tramps.

That moment marked the end of the 7:45 curtain opening, for a while at least, and the beginning of Mrs. Sexton's illness. The doctor's blue car was parked in front of her house at least once each week, usually on Monday morning at 8:00 o'clock. People said Mrs. Sexton was getting strange fevers and seeing things. People said that she had TB. But no one knew for sure. Children stopped setting their watches by her curtain opening and closing. Some Fifth Formers had become disoriented, getting to school late, and giving as the excuse, "I couldn't get my watch set right." They never gave a reason why. They did not need to.

One year passed. Then two. The First Formers who had started wearing the brown and cream had become serious Third Formers. Most students had forgotten that anyone had ever worn white uniforms to Miss Langley's School. When someone referred to the school as Miss Pickard's School, the little ones would look up with a big question in their eyes. Miss Pickard?

Eventually, Mrs. Sexton's health recovered and the new First Formers began setting their watches at her curtain openings again. She gradually began to return to church on Sunday morning, in gloves that were now a little loose, covering fingers that trembled just a little. She now walked with a cane that tapped along Oxford Street just a little slowly. Her back was bent visibly now, and the head of hair was a bleached white. But life went on, and Mrs. Sexton got accustomed to the brown and cream on the left side of the road and the khaki and white on the right. That is how it would always be. Yes Sir. Making ladies out of those girls. Ladies for the Factory homes and the homes up the Fort. All was not lost.

When Mrs. Sexton pulled her curtain open the next September, however, her frail body collapsed on the divan near the window. Her breath came in short gasps, and a short cry, like that of a hurt animal came from her frail lips. She grasped her cane and tried to close the curtain. But she fell to the floor with a weak thud.

Outside, girls in brown and cream hurried up the road at 7:45 to Miss Langley's School. Boys in khaki and white hastened up to the grammar school. Together. The left side of the road and the right side of the road were identical. Brown and cream was touching the khaki and white. Mrs. Sexton could hear the laughter and talk about Latin and French, Algebra and Geometry. Mrs. Sexton had seen one girl holding hands with a boy. Lying on the floor, she tried to fan herself, to wipe the beads of perspiration that had broken out on the wrinkled brow.

As the girls from Miss Langley's School and the boys from Grammar School returned home that afternoon walking on any side of the street they chose, they saw the doctor's blue car and an ambulance outside Mrs. Sexton's home for the last time.

Mrs. Sexton was buried later that week in her silk gloves, her white gingham dress, and her white bonnet. Rumor said that as she died she was saying something about "Factory" and "Miss Pickard." They say that her last words were "ladies," and that she kept repeating this over and over again, as she slipped fitfully away.

Today, Mrs. Sexton's house remains on Oxford Street—deserted. Creeping Ivy quietly grows on weathered walls. Fragments of curtains blow from the open holes where spotless glass frames used to shine. The wooden door is shut, with a bar over it. That bar, now rusted, swings: a pendulum without its clock. Moss and weeds contend for space in the once-trim garden. And outside, on the sidewalk, from September to July, the parade of students passes by, in shades of brown and cream, and khaki and white, together.

4.

"Forty Years On..."

Remember when
I was the pride of Oxford Street?
My polished halls welcomed
Lords and British nobles
And winding staircase saw their ladies
Glide slowly down in satin robes.
My rafters heard the clink of polished silver
As tables filled up fast for those high teas
And strong oak walls absorbed the smell
Of fresh scones, Yorkshire Pudding and Rissoles.
Remember when...
My sundial told the crowd of revelers
That the evening shades were drawing quickly in
And garden parties must stop quickly...
The governor's ball was scheduled to begin
Remember when?
But decades passed...
My polished halls had lost some of their luster
As girls in white, then brown and cream marched in
Each day for morning worship
In neat rows, singing lusty songs
And reading daily prayers
From common prayer book
Now long gone
Decades passed...
And conduct marks dispatched the bad
Up winding stairs to office of Head mistress
And reprimands to head or strokes to hand
Were given. This is what I had become—
A school where fourteen forty
Bought instruction for one term.
Now my lawns were trampled with the feet

Of young girls who had come
To learn their Latin verbs
Where Red house fought with Blue house
For each trophy, hard-won.
Decades passed...
Miss Pickard and Miss Langley
Then Miss Byron, one by one,
Did the job and led the chorus of
"Follow up, Follow up, Forty years on."

Now look at me...
The shame of Oxford Street.
My lawns sprout weeds and wild untended plants.
My outdoor garden is a forest now.
Knarled flamboyant trees
Show untrimmed growth like grey old men
My roof is gone...
Caved in by raging fire—
That took my hall and polished, gleaming walls.
My staircase is a tangle of black sticks
A danger to the feet, the eyes, the heart.
Look at me, my bronze sundial gone,
Upturned and buried deep in mounds of thrash
That fill my middle lawn, upper lawn
That fill me up...
Just look what I've become!

Yet, sometimes on a starry night
I think I hear the servants bringing trays
To lords and nobles seated in the splendor
Of my own gleaming hall.
Some bright mornings
I think I see the girls in their white clothes
With ink spots splashed on skirts or clean white socks
Sometimes I hear the sounds of morning prayer
And then I feel my old walls ring

And my trees shake
And my stairs creak—
"Follow up, Follow up, Follow up...,
Forty years on." *

* Note: The school song for Basseterre Girls School from 1950-1969 began with the words "Forty years on" and ended with the words "Follow up." Girls High School (East Campus and St. Kitts Nevis Grammar School (West Campus) became Basseterre High School. A fire destroyed the West campus in the 1970's.

5.

One for the Road

If he could have only one more drink—one for the road. That was all Morris could think of as he staggered out of the rum shop near Baker's Corner. He hated to leave, but even with his numbed mind, he knew he should be getting home. It was "pitch dark" on that November evening, for darkness comes early near the time of the winter solstice. He remembered that his geography teacher, nicknamed "Peas," had drilled that fact about the solstice into the third form, more by force than by will.

Morris knew that he should have been home long ago. With just one more year to before his O-levels, he needed to study. His last report card was a trophy—top marks in history, geography, literature, and arithmetic. High marks in physics, Latin, and algebra. Not one low score. Not one. Every teacher's comment had been similar: "Parent should be proud of your work...Great potential...Keep this up." His mother, with no more than a Standard Seven certificate herself, had hugged him roughly, unaccustomed to showing much affection. Morris had tried to return his mother's unaccustomed embrace. That close to her, he could smell the Bay Rum, the sweat, and the blue laundry soap combined. He knew that as a domestic his mother slaved all day. He was glad that she, who was father and mother to him, was proud of her first child.

But now she must be home and she would be worried. She may have sent his younger brother to look for him. That is why he had chosen a new rum shop this time. His brother would be looking for him on Market Street. Good for Boy-boy. A fella must be able to have some fun. Fun with his friends, the only friends he had, the best friends in the world. Only friends would let him drain their rum bottles, and sip from their whiskey mugs. These were true friends. Not like those grammar school boys. Sissies, Antimen—they did not know how to have a good time like a man.

Morris staggered into the street. His must remember to con-
jugate those five Latin verbs first and then do geography. He had
to create a travel chart that showed all routes from London to
New York by sailboat, or something. He really must be getting
home. Tomorrow he had a football game, and Red House had
faith in their best tackle. He could never let his team down. In the
twilight, Baker's Corner was quiet, but not empty. The bakery
was still doing a brisk business, as people bought shilling bread,
penny loaves, and buns for the next day. The bakery gave out the
warm aroma of freshly baked bread, but Morris could not smell
it. His nostrils had become accustomed to the whiskey, Vat 90,
and the rum. Morris opened his bookbag and checked his note-
book. Yes. He could spare another five minutes, so he loosened
his grammar school tie and turned right back into the rum shop.
Just one more drink with his friends. One for the road.

He had to step over one man who had passed out near the
door. The fool. A man must know how to hold his liquor. Even a
young man like Morris knew that. He could never let himself get
like this man or like the one he had seen in the gutter the previous week. Dressed in car-tire shoes and dirty pants, that man
had clutched the flat to his chest even as the brown, filthy gutter
water on Cayon Street washed over him. The schoolboys
laughed at him as they passed:

"He could have asked us to 'head' water for him to bathe. He
did not have to take a street bath."

Morris had joined the other boys in laughing. That man was
a real "rummer" and an idiot, too. People said that the man in
the gutter, Lionel, had been a "brain" at Grammar School a few
years before. He was in line for the LIS, the prestigious Leeward
Islands Scholarship. If he had not become a drunkard, Morris
heard people say, he would have been a doctor, now, or a lawyer.
What an idiot!

Now as Morris stepped over the drunkard in the rum shop,
he smiled to himself. He would never let himself become like
that man. He was, after all a Grammar School boy. "Principia,

non Homines" was his school motto. That meant that a real man would put his principles first. And Morris's principles told him that he must never get drunk to the point of passing out on the floor or in the gutter. His principles also told him that a real man must spend time in the saloon (*rum shop* sounded too vulgar) with his friends. But Morris was already staggering.

"Wha chu come back for, eh? "he heard his former neighbor at the bar ask him. "A thought chu was going home chu do yo homwok." As the man said this, he passed his nearly empty glass to Morris.

"A jus wan to get me head clear to do me home wok," Morris replied to the roar of laughter in the crowded bar. At a certain point of inebriation, any word that a comrade says is a huge joke, one for the books, the cloudy minds would insist. Their nebulous heads saw the boy as a companion, an initiate, almost, and they felt it their responsibility to show him how to "hold his likker."

The jokes became louder as the clock ticked. Then one by one the men either passed out on the floor or staggered out of the smelly room. Passers-by hurried on, or crossed to the other side of the road for fear of the smell or the loud jokes. Many feared to see a familiar face in the room or to step over someone they knew.

Inside, Morris had long ago dropped his bag with his Latin homework and his geography notes. His tie was off and had found its way to the floor. But he felt a superior sense of composure. Those idiots on the floor—they did not know how to hold their likker. They had to learn to be a man like him. He would go home, do his homework, eat his dinner, and go to sleep. This was the way to live, Man. He must keep his marks up. So many people told him that he was smart enough to get the LIS one day. Then he could go to the University of the West Indies in Jamaica to become a medical doctor. Morris knew he could make excellent marks and still spend time with his friends in the saloon. He would leave football and pole vaulting to those "antimen" at his school.

"Well, I think I'm going, now" he tried to say. Though Morris did not fully realize it, the entire sentence was a garbled grunt.

Miss Herbert, his English teacher, would have had a fit it she had heard him.

"Speak clearly if you want to be understood," she always said. And she wanted him to be on the Debating Team. "You speak so well," she constantly encouraged him.

As Morris got up to go, the floor rose to meet him. Great! That way, a man did not even have to walk. He could lie down and roll to his destination. Morris imagined himself floating on clouds up Cayon Street, to Market Street, to Dorset Village, and home. What a life!

He tried to find the door, but he kept bumping into people and things. The idiots. Why did they not put things in their places? His mother always said, "A place for everything, and everything in its place." Those people in the rum shop could learn a lot from his mother.

Morris finally felt fresh air on his face and realized that he was outside. How good it felt to be floating, rolling home. A person did not need a car, or a bicycle, or even legs. What a life! And this was just Monday. There was a whole week of drinking to do. Morris started floating home, past clouds, and pillows, and streams. This was delicious. A good drink after school should be mandatory, (from the Latin verb mandare, to order) he thought. Yes, mandatory.

That night, worried policemen and a distraught mother tried to retrace the steps Morris might have taken on his way home. Friends had seen him go into the rum shop, they said, and the shopkeeper said, ashamedly, that he had allowed the boy to stay. "I thought he was with his uncle," the shopkeeper lied. But the boy could not be found.

Tuesday dawned with a brilliant sunrise. In the crisp morning air, shopkeepers opened shop. The milkman made his rounds. The smell of bush tea and scrambled eggs woke up schoolboys and girls across Basseterre. Morris, however, had not yet come home. As his mother stepped outside to continue her search, she heard the street sweeper pushing the green moss ahead of him down the road. As he sang to himself while doing the dirty job, the mother heard the man stop and give a low whistle.

"Is what dis I see? That ain't you boy, Miss Joseph? Look how he lying in the dirty gutter like a rummer! He dead? "

But the boy was not dead.

The schoolboys that had gathered around on their way to school, the mother with swollen eyes, and the street sweeper gazed into the awakening eyes of the boy. A boy who just knew he could keep his likker, who had had a great time with his friends and who had floated home on a pillowy street that had come to meet him. A boy who was sure he had done his home-work, who had slept a sweet sleep on a firm green bed, and who had taken a long delicious bath in brown, flowing water. His clothes were soaking wet with some brown stuff, and a hammer seemed to be pounding at his head, but he had learned to hold his likker. His friends would be proud of him.

6.

The Man and The Child

He had strong sinewy limbs—the limbs of a cane cutter. His muscles had grown strong and firm from years of cutting the annual crop of sugar cane at Parsons Estate. His face had grown hard through years in the sun at cane-cutting time, for even as a child he had cut cane to support the family. In the absence of a father, a big brother had to take care of his mother and the little ones, and Manny did, without complaint.

The hard work had matured the boy into a man, quickly. Manny could calculate compound interest on the loan to Mr. Bailey's shop where the family got "trust" to buy food when the cane season was "off." Manny could figure out how much was owed and how many "hands" of cane he would have to cut when the crop began to pay off the debt. However, writing and reading always gave him trouble. But he could make his X like any man when he had to sign for his week's pay.

Manny knew that his younger brothers and sisters would read and write, though. Manny was sure of that. They would go to Teacher Walwyn's School up by the Moravian Church. They would go to school in clean flourbag shirts and pants. They didn't need shoes or socks, and one dress or pair of pants could last most of the year. Paulette was the only one who gave trouble for clothes. She grew like a gourd vine in the rainy season. The band to her waist would be up below her breasts in no time, and she would have to stay at home until Mama could get another flourbag to sew her a dress. Manny knew that his nine brothers and sisters would have it easier than he did. Yes, Siree. Life would be different for them. If only there was cane to cut more than once a year!

When the cane-cutting season was over, Manny would go to school, Teacher Walwyn's School up by the Moravian Church. There he was the biggest boy in Standard Three. The boys his age and size were way up in Standard Six. Manny looked awkward in the little Standard Three benches. His knees would knock the desk and sometimes turn the whole thing over.

The Standard Three children would always laugh at Manny. "Manny writing look like crab foot running down de road." "Manny, spell *cat*. No not *man*. Manny, you can't even spell *cat*. You dunce like a crab!"

Manny would bow his head and clench his fists under the desk. If he weren't so big, he would cry. He would feel the hot tears back of his eyes, but he could not let them fall. In the one-room school there was no privacy, and if Manny cried, he would have the whole school laughing at him. If only he could be smart and read out of the Caribbean Reader. Some of the Third Standard girls were reading from the Standard Five Reading Book already, but Manny could hardly figure out *c a t* from the Standard One Primer.

At recess, Manny played ball with the bigger boys. The game was fast, hard, and Manny with his strong muscles was a clear favorite. He wished recess would last all day. But soon the recess bell rang, and Teacher Walwyn was at the door waiting for the children to line up to go back to their classrooms.

Manny always hated those lines. Why did he always feel like a lonely coconut tree on Dieppe Bay Beach? He could look down on the heads of all the boys and girls around him." Dummy! Moomoo!" his height seemed to be screaming at him. No one had to say a word.

The next class was Reading. Instinctively, Manny clenched his fists at the thought. He must learn his letters today. *B* and *D* always mixed him up. He shook his head as if shaking would dispel the confusion he knew would come in a few minutes. He noticed his teacher looked at the class waiting quietly before her on the hard, wooden benches, benches that still smelled of the dettol and blue soap they had been scrubbed with just three days before. Manny realized that she took pride in her class, and in her corner of the one-room school. She also took pride in those students, those nappy-headed boys and girls. He wanted her to be proud of him, her biggest student. He shuffled uncomfortably in the small, tight seat. The routine spelling of the words from yesterday's lesson had begun. Children from the front row were taking turns spelling the words. One by one the children rose as their names were called, and they politely called out the letters before sitting down. Manny was becoming nervous. Three more boys before him. Then two. He sighed. Perhaps he would get an easy word. When he looked up, he teacher was staring directly at him:

"Manny, spell *school*."

School? He could remember *sand* and *safe*, but *school*?

"Manny, did you hear what I said? I said spell *school, school*. We learned it yesterday. Don't you remember?"

The teacher's words seemed like nettles in a sugar cane field, cutting through tender flesh, embedding themselves and digging further in. She was waiting. They were all waiting for him to spell school.

"S k ——."

Manny did not get beyond that letter. His classmates were giggling softly behind their hands. He knew that he was wrong, again. He could imagine the children whispering, "Manny dunce like a crab, like a crab, a crab."

Suddenly, Manny could take it no longer. He lashed out at the boy next to him, and the child fell heavily to the wooden floor. Manny went after the screaming child, pounding him with his steel-like muscles, those cane cutting machines that fed a family and put clothes on their backs. Pinned to the floor, the boy could offer no resistance, but Manny fought as if for his own survival—blindly. Blood flowed from a gash over the boy's upper lip and his shirt was torn, exposing the child's bony back.

Manny felt someone pulling at his shoulders, his hands, pulling him away, but he could see nothing but the rage and the Standard Three Reader larger than a man now before him. He kept lashing until his hands were pinned behind his back, and he saw Teacher Walwyn standing in front of him.

"Come to the platform, Manny. I will have to punish you. You almost killed the boy. You couldn't see he is a child to you?

You don't have any respect for your teacher and the rest of the school? I will have to punish you right now."

Manny followed the headmaster to the platform. He could feel the laughter coming from the silent faces of the whole school. He passed Standard One, where his little sisters were. Manny did not meet their eyes. He walked right up to the platform where Teacher Walwyn was already taking out his leather belt. It was not the belt the headmaster wore around his waist, but The Belt, the one that lay in salt water until the headmaster was ready for it. Manny had seen boys and girls go up to the platform for licks. He knew the stinging sound when the wet, salty belt fell on a child's back, but he had never felt it. Wiping the excess water from the belt, the teacher spoke harshly to the boy:

"Face the platform, Manny, and look at me. This is a school, not a rum shop. Do you think you are drunk, beating up a little child like that? You are two times his size. You ought to be ashamed of yourself. I am going to make an example of you. If anyone boy in this school thinks he can do something like this, look at what Manny is going to get and remember. You will get a dozen lashes, Manny, a dozen."

On the platform, the teacher stood facing the school. Every class had ceased working. Teachers stood respectfully by, chalk in hand. Pupils sat motionless on the wooden benches, scrawny hands resting on the rough wood before them, eyes straining to see the beating that would take place. With his back to the rest of the school, the boy faced the teacher, his eyes coming level with the teacher's hands whose fingers curled around the still dripping belt. Manny did not look up to see the teacher's face but saw and heard the swish as the belt was raised.

The belt descended once.

Manny did not move. He could not let them see him feel it. And actually, he hardly felt it. His back had become used to the blows of the midday sun. It could take a lot.

Two
Three
Four

Manny was beginning to feel the blows now. A sodden, leather belt could do real damage. His back began to feel sore, then raw.

Five.

Manny opened his mouth in a wrenching scream as the belt came down, and leaping in pain felt his teeth close over the soft flesh of the headmaster's hand. The salty taste of fresh blood and the harsh feel of sinews shocked him, and he opened his mouth.

But the damage had been done. Teacher Walwyn was tearing off his shirt and wrapping his bloody hand in it. His right thumb was hanging at a strange angle.

Everywhere, there were children running, screaming. Teachers were rushing to the platform, holding Teacher Walwyn's hand, begging someone to call Nurse Walwyn to come look for her husband.

Manny sat outside on the steps of the school and heard the commotion inside. All the "Man" had been drained out of him and he felt like the little boy he really was. A frightened little boy. He would learn to read, he knew, and write. One day he would write a letter to Teacher Walwyn and tell him how sorry he was for biting his hand. Yes. He would learn to write.

But now he was ready to face the school—like a man—and take the rest of his licks.

Snapshot

7.

Crazy Mano

They call me Crazy Mano, but my real name is Prince Alphonso Alfredo Manitvani. And I would like to know why these people of St. Kitts run from me and say that I am demented. It is true that I do not work at a traditional job. But I do have a job—a very important job. I work for my father, the king of Afhuti. You may never have heard of that kingdom, but that does not say it does not exist. I am an ambassador to St. Kitts for my father, and some day you St. Kitts people will recognize the signal importance of my presence in your country and be ashamed.

Where do I live, you ask? I reside in a small cottage in the hills back of Shadwell in the town of Basseterre. It is only a piece of tarpaulin over some tree trunks you say? That's all right. Laugh at me if you will. Now you have seen my subterfuge. I am learning to live like the common people in my kingdom of Asbunfi. And what do I do about food? If you have seen me eating out of the thrash cans, be assured that I look for only the best discarded material. I am a prince, and only the best must go into my royal system.

If I look dirty to you, that is only a matter of perception. What is dirt but organic material? On my body and my clothes that material is being transposed into enzymes and organisms that replenish and feed my system. In a few years my father's kingdom will be the one to lead the world in the use of reabsorbed and recycled particles from skin and clothes. The whole world will follow our lead in this scientific breakthrough.

So if you don't like how I smell or how I look, don't worry. In a few years, you'll all be looking and smelling like me. Then you'll bow down to your majesty, me, and be ashamed.

It is almost three o'clock by my royal sundial. I need to walk to Warner Park up Victoria Road. The cricket match between the West Indies and Australia is in full swing. So the thrash cans should be full of half eaten chicken bones and parts of penny loaves. I'm feeling hungry. Look at those children from Miss Sebastian's school holding their noses. I laugh at them. I pity them for thinking I am mad!

"*Crazy Mano? Crazy Mano? I'll show you Crazy Mano.*" I'll just wave my hand at my subjects.

"*I'm the monarch of all I survey. Don't run, children, don't run. I know you say that St. Kitts is full of crazy people. I think so too. Look at Cockeriko and DoDoBim. But I am not crazy. I am a Prince, a Prince, I say. Stop throwing stones at me. I am not a common hound!*"

If they keep this up, I'll indeed chase them and make them think I'm really daft.

"*Avanut, thou foolish ones, Avanut. You're mocking me? You all go ahead. My father, the king, will have all of you beheaded. Beheaded, I tell you.*"

I had forgotten that school is out at this time, or I would never have come here. Those Grammar School boys think they are hot stuff because they know Latin and French. Well, I can speak a little of another language too.

"*Aprocijy digeimh Hve hve.*"

See I can talk foreign language, too. Not because Miss Katzen didn't teach it to me. I'll have to teach it to her.

"*Aohicup Aohidup, Ha! And all you stop calling me Crazy Mano before I really turn crazy on all you.*"

Let me hide in this alley till those Grammar School boys have gone. They don't want me to show my royal power. I know I can decimate them in an instant. Let me restrain myself from abuse of power. Now my belly is killing me. I need to get my repast. When those boys have gone, I'll see what the thrash cans will provide for today's meal.

Perhaps I'll go to the Pentecostal Church since I have had my afternoon rest. I hear they having special service this week. Eh Eh, you know it is late. The mosquito and them start to bite. I better hurry before the service is all finished. I like those pretty Richards' girls in that church. I am thinking of asking one of them to become my wife, my princess. She will be the queen of my new kingdom.

"What you church people running for? You don't hear the preacher preaching?"

Oh, good. They leave all these seats for me. Look how that old woman is retreating to the rear of the building. I thought I heard she had arthritis. I believe it is my humble presence that has revitalized her. You St. Kitts people will thank me one of these days for all I have done for you.

"Go, ahead, Preacher. Preach to me. Preach!"

I wonder why that preacher ran out of the church so fast? I thought he was going to fall down those platform steps. He disappeared so rapidly that it seems he had wings. Do you see the effect I have on people? If I were a crazy man, people would not get so much strength when they see me. I have seen old men throw away their walking sticks and run as fast as that Berridge boy at Sports Day. I have seen blind people fly round some corners. It is my royal power.

Anybody know what part of the church that Richards' girl is hiding...the one with the curly hair? She must know that she's the chosen one. I want to propose to her tonight. Tonight, before I get...

"Policeman, remove your hands from my royal body, and stop making up you all faces as if you all smell something bad. You don't know that you should be bowing down to my royal feet? You want me to come to the crazy house, you say? You going to put me in a straight jacket?

You better find a crazy house big enough for all of you, for I am the sanest, the smartest, and the most important person on this island. Go look for Cockeriko and DodoBim and all them other crazy people. I am the Prince of Ambusi. I am conducting scientific experiments for the Federal Government of my Kingdom. I am..."

8.

St. Kitts People

If you think you see everything in the world, I willing to bet you something. You never see people run from rain like St. Kitts people. Look me crosses. If a drizzle start to fall, Barcley's Bank shut down. Bata close. The people say they 'fraid they catch "fresh cold." I don't think any place in the whole world have more fresh cold than St. Kitts.

And they say that is fresh cold does lead to TB. You ever pass by the TB ward where the old hospital was near the cemetery? Man, all you hearing is "Kuf, Kuf, Kuf," and "Aheng, Aheng."

And whatever you do, don't pass by the hospital window, for the TB people like to cough and spit out of the window, not for spite, mind you, but you may be passing at the wrong time. I don't know why anyone would put a TB ward right beside a street, but is St. Kitts people you talking 'bout.

I from St. Kitts too, but you would think how I talking that I come from Anguilla. Not that I don't like my people and them, but I like to talk straight, even if all you St. Kitts people don't like me.

And that was why I didn't go to Brimstone Hill Easter Monday. Now, I like to make joke just like anybody else, but I don't make no joke with rain. I ain't taking no chance with TB, I telling you. I have no plans of spending the rest of my life in no TB ward, even though I hear they does get plenty ice cream and Jell-O in there. I don't know what ice cream and Jell-O have to do with making TB people better, but, as I tell you, is St. Kitts people you talking 'bout.

I hear they planning big break away up Brimstone Hill for Easter. They going to have calypso, and steel band and thing, but they going to have rain, too, I hear, and as I tell you I ain't taking no chance with me health. I staying home. I going pound a few stones down by the bay. If I ain't going to Brimstone Hill, I might as well make some money. What you think? So I down by the bay keeping my humbrella near and watching them clouds. I ain't taking no chance. No Sir.

Man, I see the sun like it burning bright for spite, and I getting more and more vexed with meself. I here asking meself why I didn't take a chance and go to Brimstone Hill. I can imagine all my friends drinking coconut water and eating tart and sugar cake. And I here getting me fingers and them pound because I can't even concentrate on the stone and the pounding. But still I comforting myself telling myself I ain't getting no TB. Not me, Sir.

Then I feel the first drop. Mearm, the sun still shining. I ain't know where the rain come from. Before I could grab me humbrella and run, man I down, soaking wet. The sun still shining and they say that when sun shine and rain fall it is the Devil beating his wife. She must be getting some blows, for that rain coming for spite.

Man, I run leave stone, everything. When I reach home and take off me clothes, I just remember them people up Brimstone Hill. I think of all them girls who press they hair, and now the rain must have catch them. I want to laugh, but I only thinking 'bout them catching TB. And I can't laugh no more.

By time I take off me wet clothes and look outside, the rain stop just so. But is so St. Kitts rain does fall. Hard and short. Before you look, it finish.

I eat me dinner and fall asleep right there by the settee. I might as well get some pleasure out of me holiday. Tomorrow I have to go cut cane again.

When I wake up I hear the steel band and the calypso. That mean that the people coming back from Brimstone Hill. I look out of the window and see them down soaking wet and dancing in the band. I don't know if is sweat or rain, but they don't seem to mind.

But I ain't even studying them. I taking care of me health, you see? I ain't getting no wet and I ain't catching no TB. No Siree. But I bawl out and ask me neighbor if they had plenty rain up Brimstone Hill. 'Cause I sure I going get to laugh at them. My neighbor can hardly hear me. He jumping up so hard in de band. So he answer:

"Rain? What rain you talking 'bout? We ain't see a drop up Brimstone Hill. You all had rain down here?"

He ain't even waiting for me to answer. He and the band going down the road. But is now I feeling foolish. I sneezing as if a fresh cold coming on, and the worst part is that if anyone going to catch TB, is me.

9.

Hot Sand

Moonlight streamed through the open windows of the living room at Conaree Estates, turning everything to magical silver. Now that the sun had set, a cool tropical breeze blew directly on the face of the mother. Yet Monica fanned herself briskly. She did not feel the cool breeze. Or see the moonlight. Through red eyes she was reading, again, the letter her son had brought home from school:

"Dear Parent,

We regret to inform you ..."

She did not need to read any more. She now knew the letter by heart. Charlie had struck the Physics teacher, Mr. Webb. His mother must accompany him to school to meet with his teachers the following day. A decision had to be made about this "incorrigible" young man. The principal noted that, although Charlie had claimed it was an accidental blow, the incident was not isolated. The time had come for serious decisions to be made about his future at the school.

Monica thought of the six other letters which she had received from the school since the academic year had started. Charlie was a disruptive influence in the class. He was rude to his math teacher, again. Every week brought another letter, another complaint. Charlie would read the letter with his mother and explain everything. Some stupid boy had looked at him wrong. Somebody had stepped on his brand-new shoes. A guy must protect himself. A child had teased him about how he spoke, about his accent, as if he could help it. There was always an excuse. It was never his fault. And still the letters came. Charlie's mother had tried talking to the teachers on the telephone. That had sporadically produced some good results. But Charlie had no excuse for the fight with Mr. Webb. The man had a black eye to prove it. Charlie was lucky that he had not been arrested.

41

Now his mother would have to accompany him to school tomorrow. Assaulting a teacher was criminal. This was real trouble. Monica practiced the words she might use at the meeting: "I really try with him. I teach him to be respectful. You know how I feel about discipline. I feel so embarrassed. I mean, he is sixteen years old. Charlie is not a child anymore. I do not know what to do."

Monica got up from her seat feeling twenty years older. She looked at the clock and was shocked to see that it was already eleven o'clock. Was her son still awake?

Charlie was fast asleep with a book in his hand, looking like the innocent child his mother remembered. If only he could behave as well as he could read! How is it that a boy who could discuss the political situations in every European country did not understand the consequences of rudeness?

Today's visit to the school would be so much unlike the first visit the mother had made to the school. Monica tried to dismiss the pleasant memories from her mind and prepared to face tomorrow. Yet she could not forget those words that had inspired each parent and she would always remember the response of the teachers—a response that had earned the speaker a new job, the highest job in the Department of Education—the job of superintendent. At that time dealing with a teenager seemed such a joy. It had seemed almost an adventure.

Like any mother, however, Monica had dreams as well as nightmares—a top of the plate experience and bottom of the plate experience. Hadn't the speaker said those words? Tomorrow would be the nightmare, the bottom of the plate and Monica did not need it. If only the dreams would remain. If only the beautiful top of the plate would show. Monica did not need the embarrassment, or the stress.

The long night dragged on as Monica grasped her pillows. One lonely mosquito buzzed in her ear. Was this empathy? Was that mosquito the parent of a teen-aged insect? Monica, usually angered by the tropical creatures like lizards, woodslaves, and centipedes, was unruffled by this one, considering it a fellow sufferer. In the distance a lonely cock crowed, and a donkey brayed. Monica heard each lonely sound. She also saw the crescent moon outlining every object in the room, highlighting every detail. Wide-awake, she thought:

Suppose she did not go to that meeting tomorrow? Suppose she only called to talk to the teachers as she did before? But the principal would be there in the meeting also. This was serious business.

Suppose she took sick tomorrow? The thought was more than tempting. But Monica knew she could not be ill forever. Like a crab, she had to face the sand one day. She could not stay underground forever. And when the crab came out, the sand would be waiting for it, and the sand would be hot!

When Monica awoke the next morning, the warm Caribbean sun was already streaming into the window. Monica loved it. It was the sun and the beaches that had made her fall in love with the island of St. Kitts in the first place. Nearby the sea at Conaree Beach pounded, and Monica could see the white spray high in the air. This was home. But for how long after today she did not know. She dressed thoughtfully, as if for the last time, as one dresses for one's own funeral. She chose the colors of the pleated skirt and silk blouse with care.

Should she use the jeep today or ... Perhaps not, she decided against the alternative. Charlie was now dressed, finishing the last chapters of *The Killing Ground*, but with no school books in sight.

"Sorry Ma," the boy spoke softly. " I did not think...."

"That's the problem. You never think. It's always I'm sorry Mom. When will you use that thing between your two ears? When? Tell me."

The boy was silent.

"Charlie, you know how hard I'm trying. You promised me..."

Avoiding the potholes on the dirt road took all of Monica's concentration for the next several minutes, so for a while the two drove in silence, each hoping that the ride would never end. On the way Monica looked at the scores of children walking singly or in groups, clutching their bags or books. Some had lunch kits. The others would take the long trek home again at noon and return for one o'clock. All were neat and clean, and in uniform— blue and beige, green and gold, tunics with three pleats over white blouses. Even after three months that sight still impressed Monica, and she sighed deeply.

Monica and Charlie waited in the jeep while the other students rushed into the school before the late bell sounded. They sat quietly in the hot vehicle until Charlie broke the silence.

"I'm so sorry, Ma. I don't know what's wrong with me. These people just don't like me. I wish——"

"Wish what? That you had not messed up my life? That I had not brought you with me? What do you want me to do? You are my only child."

The woman bit her lip before she said anything else. She had pressed her teeth together so firmly that she tasted blood. She bent her head over the steering wheel; she remembered the night of his conception, as she satisfied her need for company. She hardly knew the man, just someone she had met at the party. There she was, thirty-five years of age, single, and drunk. When she woke up the next morning, vomiting, she knew something momentous had happened. She had borne the pregnancy with resignation, dealing with the disappointment of her aging parents and the loss of income because ill health had consumed all her sick time. But she held out the hope, perhaps this is the child who will make up for all those lonely years. I will have someone to call my own. She remembered giving birth alone, with no mother to soothe and no husband to comfort. Charlie was her child and she would show the world what a great mother she would be.

"Please don't go in there, Ma. Please. I'll quit school. I'll go back..."

Her son's urging brought Monica back to reality. But she put her head down again. Yesterday was better, when he was just a baby, just a cute little kid. She would show the world. Yes, her son was going to display all that was finest in child rearing. That was yesterday.

44

"Ma, are you even listening to me? You are looking off into space somewhere. You don't have to go in there. Let's just leave."

The mother seemed to agree with the son. She placed polished fingers on the keys in the ignition as if starting the car, as if she would drive away from this place and never look back. But instead, she took the keys out of the ignition and opened the door resolutely, before she could change her mind.

The well-dressed woman was graciously ushered to the principal's office as the young man followed at at respectful distance. When the door opened for the nine o'clock appointment, Monica looked into the faces of the teachers and administrators who had gathered to help a troubled boy, her son. The flustered principal approached Dr. Peters, changing subjects like used kleenex:

"Superintendent, what a surprise! You did not tell us that you were coming for an official visit. We would have been prepared for you. Have you come to help us with this student? You must have heard about Charlie, our "incorrigible." I have never had a superintendent show so much interest in the school as you have. I can't get over that speech that you gave last Speech Day! Parents are still talking about it. We are so happy you took the job. St. Kitts needs people like you. We are waiting for Charlie's mother, a Miss Peter. Strange, almost like your name, but the opposite of you. The opposite. You may be able to help her, poor woman. Excuse me, Superintendent, while I speak to the secretary. Miss Maynard, please send Charlie Peter in with his mother."

The boy's head appeared at the door, and his body seemed more to be pushed in than to come voluntarily.

"Charlie, you are on time. Is your mother here yet? "

Without a word the tall young man shuffled into the room and walked directly to the superintendent. The looked at each other for a long, long second.

"Yes, Charlie's mother is here," said the new school superintendent, Dr. Monica Peters, as she stood beside her troubled son. "No crab can stay in its shell forever. It must face the sand someday. And I think I'm ready."

If a hurricane had blown into the room at that moment, no one would have noticed it. If a volcano had erupted, pouring its scalding lava into the room, no one would have stirred.

10.

The Silent Hibiscus

Hibiscus Street is silent today
Once there was the sound of digging and pouring
Pounding stones and laying bricks
Once there were windows placed
Tiles laid
Neighbors moving in

Hibiscus Street is quiet today
No more tired feet
And midwife's late night call
No more baby cries and toddler's steps
School bags and lunch times—
Neighbors off to school

Hibiscus Street is peaceful today
Once the sound of Bach and Haydn
Marked the break of each new day
And evening closed with joyful hymns
And prayers of father and mother
Christmas tunes and choir songs
As neighbors shared their talents

Hibiscus Street is lonely today
No more perfumed letters
With stamps from far away
No more warm nights on the front porch
With moon overhead and stars in the sky
No more wedding bells—
Children falling in love

Hibiscus street is quiet today
No more ambulance calls
And funeral trains
No more beds put far away
Nor tears nor shrieks nor one last gasp—
Neighbors going Home

Hibiscus Street is silent today
The wind blows through trees
That know it all
Saw it all
Heard it all
The wind blows and the stars shine
And the postman brings a letter
"To Grandma, with love."

From a place where there is pouring
And digging and pounding and laughter
And a new neighborhood that has just begun.

11.

Deprivation

"News flash. The ban on televisions has been upheld in a recent meeting of the House of Parliament. Anyone who breaks this ban will be subject to one year in prison with hard labor, or to a fine of..."

We hear the news on Radio Station ZIZ with leaden hearts, losing hopes for a breakthrough—for word from our state officials that we have grown up at last and can have TV in our homes in St. Kitts. After all, Antigua has TV. Even little Montserrat has TV. Visitors to St. Kitts talk about "Gilligan's Isle" and "Lucy," and we listen in silence and shame. Our government, our paid officials, do not trust us with modern entertainment. They want us to be deprived.

So we continue our accustomed fun. We go up to Sofa Stone, pushing our muscles to the limit to scale that mountain. We leave early in the morning, taking sugar cake and mauby in our bags and stopping to pick pink fatpork, mocco, ginip, and ripe brown tamarinds on our way. The bland taste of the fatpork soothes mouths lacerated with the acid tamarinds and makes us consume our small store of water too early.

We watch out for "Casha" and its many sharp prickles. We pick Jumbie Beads to take home for pitching marbles in the dirt and for Wori. Jumbie Beads are not heavy, even when our bags are full, and the dry pods make a musical shake-shake as we continue our climb. A Stinking Toe tree has ripe fruit that does not survive our attack. What Stinking Toe we do not eat we stuff into almost-full bags. We will have souvenirs to take back home with us.

The last steep part of the climb is always the worst. Two hours have passed, and feet now move mechanically, apparently without help from mind or body, determined to reach the top. Sofa Stone must be climbed all the way, or not at all.

The mountaintop is worth it, though. We compete to be first to reach the sofa-shaped stone that has given the mountain its name. There we sit feeling life return to our toes, our feet, our legs. Someone produces cool, strong ginger beer in a flask, and sandwiches.

With full stomachs and aching bodies we are ready to enjoy the view. And what a view it is. Nevis Peak towers in the distance like a broad funnel sending out slowly-rising smoke. Statia is to the right, its mountains hiding The Bottom, that strangely-named town. The Caribbean Sea forms a broad blue-green puddle around the shores of St. Kitts. Sugar cane fields like patchwork pieces slope gently to the sea shore.

Caught up in the scene, we are silent, no matter how many times we have been to Sofa Stone. Soon the green hillside and the stillness induce sleep. We awaken with lungs full of clean mountain air, ready to make the trip back in half the time.

Such is our humble entertainment.

Sleep is sweet that night, after BBC world news at seven o'clock, Greenwich Mean Time, and after bush tea and bread and cheese.

But first there is time to go to Mrs. Charles' house down the road, to sit on her porch, with the mosquitoes buzzing, and to talk.

There is time to watch the Great Dipper, and Pleiades, and Orion; time to see the shapes of the night clouds.

There is time for the new moon, or the half moon, or the full moon that turns everything to a magical silver, and time to see the fire flies in the shadows that the mango trees cast.

There is time to see my own shadow getting longer and longer the closer I go to my quiet home.

Still we Kittitians take trips abroad, to Montserrat, and Antigua, and St. Croix. We need to make up for being deprived in St. Kitts. And in another country we see "Gilligan's Island" and Lucy and News. It's fun. We like it. But we can't wait to get back home again to go down by the bay, or up to Sofa Stone, or to look for Orion and Pleiades on a quiet, quiet night.

12.

December in St. Christopher

December in St. Christopher
And a special kind of feeling
A feeling of warmth
From the rich, red sorrel trees
In crowded backyards
And the bottles of warm, blood-red sorrel drink
Spiked with ginger and cloves and anise
Ripening on the table

A feeling of wealth
As the bag of full, shelled pigeon peas
Grows heavy in the twilight
And gifts made by hands that care
Must hide
Until it's Christmas Eve.
A feeling of excitement
As new paint covers
Dingy, tired walls
And fresh linoleum gives on oily smell
On the faded kitchen floor
As windows boast their fresh, new curtains
And new tapestry revives old chairs

I step outside, and catch my breath
The Christmas breeze is blowing—
A breeze that brings the pungent smell
Of apples wrapped in light, green sheets
Of Christmas pudding boiling on the stove
Of fresh pine trees adorning spotless rooms.

The Christmas breeze blows
And gently bends the trees—
The red Poinsettias with their pointed leaves
And white Euphobias that have been green all year.

It is December in St. Christopher

Soon the Scratch Band will play
And the Mocojumbie on his stilts
Will dance with John, the Bull
On Central Street

But now, it's quiet
It's just December—
December in St. Kitts
And a special kind of feeling.

13.

A Craving
(An Ex-patriate Laments)

I'm hungry, hungry for my native fruits
Slices of cool, ripe papayas
With soft yellow flesh
And pieces of avocado-pear
Long bottleneck slices
Yellow, and green
And sweet

Hungry for rosy-cheeked mangoes
That grow on Old Road Shore
Dark pink mouthfuls
With honey for juice

Hungry for tamarind —
Ripe in dry April skies
Bunches brown and tempting on tall tamarind trees
Green tamarind, floury tamarind, ripe tamarind
So sour it cuts the roof of my mouth
I'm hungry for
Tamarind drink and stew
Tamarind balls
Just hungry for tamarind

Dying to eat fat pork
Growing wild on sloping hillsides
Fleshy and sweet and filling and good
And hungry for golden apple
That ripens in August
And bunches of ginips
That stain my good clothes

A Craving

I'm waiting for mamsiport
To make mamsiport jam,
And guava and gooseberry
So good for the stew

Look, my clothes have no stains
And my mouth's not on fire
I'm eating—or swallowing— tart
(tasteless) peaches

For my mind is not here
It's traveling, traveling
To a little paradise of tamarinds
And rosycheeks, and ginip and fatpork
With coconut and guava and sweet mamsiport,
And my heart is stuffed full
Of St. Christopher's fruits.

Across the Channel

14.

Rich Man's Toy

Nobody had to give Lucille, the young nurse from Charlestown, a second invitation to the bazaar the first week of May. At the hospital, everyone had been speaking about it for weeks. The bazaar would mean a day off from housework, from washing the drill pants, bleaching the white clothes on the stone heap in the front yard, and baking a batch of bread. The bazaar would be a day off from changing bandages and emptying bedpans at the hospital.

The bazaar would mean eating home made soursop icecream, coconut tarts, and johnnycakes. It was the place for watching children play Hoop, jump rope, and London Bridge. Lucille would get a chance to see all the new styles of boots and pinafores on display. Though she was not one to dance around the Maypole, she could watch the dancers. With all the trinkets on sale, she could not buy nice crochet pieces for her hope chest, not yet, but she could look, and dream.

At the bazaar Lucille could forget the pain of losing her mother twelve years ago and the anguish of being separated from her father and all her sisters and brothers, especially Ursulla and Henny and Son, her nephew. Son was only a baby when his grandmother died in childbirth—a handicapped baby at that, but sharp as a whistle, everyone said. Lucille, a trained nurse, felt that Son needed her. Lucille also felt that Son loved her best. Perhaps Ruth, his young mother, would allow his Aunt Ursula to bring him to the bazaar. Lucille's adopted family was good to her, but some times she still cried at nights, wanting the mother she lost when she was only nine. The bazaar would bring sweet forgetfulness.

Days before, Lucille had sewed a pretty scarf from left-over fabric. That would decorate her plain, plaited hair. She must look festive for this one day. Lucille polished her one pair of "other" shoes, and darned her one pair of cotton stockings. The stockings were old and "hand-me-down" but they were a brilliant white, just like all of Lucille's other clothes. A good bleaching in the sun, and a few sprinkles of water periodically gave clothes a white to be proud of. Lucille just knew she would look special at the annual bazaar, just like she did last year when she saw him looking at her.

Perhaps that young teacher, Darryl, would be at the bazaar with his friend, Tony, from Bath Village. Lucille knew that both young men were attracted to her. She often wondered if each knew the other did. She liked both of them too. But for Darryl there was something more, something she did not understand. Sometimes Lucille would find herself almost breathless when she thought of Darryl. Was that what people called falling in love? One day she would think of marriage, one day. But for now it was good to have someone special to dream about, to talk to, even though Mother Tailor, her adopted mother, had to be within earshot and view of Lucille every time Darryl came to visit. Mother T would sit in the rocking chair pretending to read a book. Lucille knew she was really listening to every word the two young people spoke. Lucille knew that Mother Tailor was going to the bazaar, but she would be too busy organizing the women's group and the men's activities to pay attention to Lucille. Today would be Lucille's day off indeed.

Lucille awoke exhausted on the day of the bazaar. She had tossed all that night in anticipation. Somebody had said that there would be a special treat for all who went to the bazaar. They said something about a new Ford Automobile that had just arrived in Nevis. They said that Mr. Chatterton, the richest man in Nevis, was going to try out his new Ford at the pasture where the bazaar was to be held. People from St. Kitts had talked about the first automobile in St. Kitts, bought by one Mr. Wade. St. Kitts people talked about Mr. Wade's automobile in awed voices. They spoke about the steering wheel that you had to turn to make the automobile go left or right. They mentioned that the automobile could go faster than a horse and buggy. They talked about the thing called "brakes" that the driver "held" if you wanted the thing to stop. People said it was like a horse and buggy without the horse! The whole thing sounded like obea to Lucille. Why could people not be satisfied with the horse and buggy!

It was a glorious Nevis morning. Nevis Peak seemed to have thrown off its bonnet of clouds and looked decked out in its best green frock. Everywhere, one could smell johnnycakes frying and saltfish cooking. Children were sweeping up their yards, a usual night chore, knowing full well that they would be too tired to sweep it that evening. The blue-green water of Nevis harbor was peaceful today. That water could turn up and flood Main Street in Charlestown during bad weather, but today the waves seemed to be almost asleep.

In the Tailor household, the food was already packed into large wicker baskets, covered with clean, starched towels. The two little girls wore pink ribbons in their hair. The boys had been coaxed into short pantsuits with black ties. Mother Tailor put away her dark, formal dress for the day and wore a yellow flowing chiffon dress. She hardly looked like the same person. Father Tailor's face boasted a relaxed smile. Everyone smelled good from the Dixie Peach and the Eau-de-cologne.

"We going to have horse race today, Daddy?" asked David, the youngest boy.

"No, son," his preacher father replied. "Today we going see the Automobile Ford."

"What Dat?"

"What is that" his father corrected him. "That is a thing like a horse and buggy. It has a buggy, but it does not have a horse."

"Well how dat ting run? Eh, Daddy? How dat run?"

"Say *that thing*, Child, and don't let me have to tell you again to speak properly. That Thing as you call it runs with petrol from a bottle. I don't see how it can work, but I hear that America has a lot of them. Don't bother to ask me for one. They are the rich man's toys and your father is a poor preacher."

By noon the bazaar was in full swing. Most men and women had retreated from the heat of the sun to the shady ginip trees that bordered the pasture. Men played dominoes in the shade, and the braver ones attempted to start a cricket match despite the May Day heat. Women in pretty scarves served warm food from steaming pans and talked about the latest birth in Charlestown, and about the biting insects, Granny Nippers. Sales of crocheted doilies and pillowcases were brisk. Things were going well. But quietly everyone was on the lookout for one thing: the automobile, the Ford. They talked about it as one talks about Antarctica or the fabled city, Atlantis.

"You think Mr. Chadderton know how to drive that thing? I hear it ain't have no harness like the horse and buggy."

"I hear Mr. Chadderton done hire himself somebody from St. Kitts to drive him around."

"I wonder if Mrs. Chatterton going drive in that thing?"

"If she don't go, she stupid. She husband buy a big New York Ford, and she going cut styles? If it was me nobody would have to invite me. I woulda be in dey as soon as the thing land down by the pier."

"I hear it take bout fifty men to hoist that thing offer the boat."

"You hear fifty, well I hear it take two times that."

"You always zaggerating."

And so the talk and speculation tossed back and forth and the sun made its way across the clear sky.

Lucille, with Son at her side, was busy keeping an eye on the Tailor children, but not too busy for Darryl who had found her soon after he had arrived. It was not prudent for a young man and a young woman to be seen alone, so they mingled with everyone, but had eyes only for each other. Darryl's friend, Tony, paced around sucking his teeth loudly. The girl that he loved and his best friend seemed to be courting. Tony suck teeth grew louder and more convincing as the afternoon wore on. Lucille was the girl for him. Why was he so slow to act? Now he may have lost her forever. Perhaps he could find someone else for Darryl. Perhaps...

Suddenly, a sound like an erupting volcano interrupted the merriment. All eyes were riveted in the direction of a cloud of dust near the entrance to the park. The pace bowler froze, the ball dropping silently at his feet. The bang bang of dominoes ceased. Children hiding in the game of Hide and Seek suddenly appeared. Several voices screamed:

"Look, it coming. It coming full speed. The Ford Automobile. All you get out of the way."

The warning came too late. Like a steamer cutting through the water at the Channel, a huge black monster with four wheels barged into the crowd of children playing hoop in the pasture.

Lucille screamed as she saw a boy in a red shirt go under its wheels.

"Son, Son. Lord save him," she cried, thinking of her handicapped nephew.

But Son was beside her.

Women and men were scrambling into the nearby ginip trees, holding on to branches. Children's muffled cries could be heard from under the Ford. It had not stopped coming toward the crowd.

Inside the black monster, two men could be seen moving their hands feverishly. One seemed to be looking for harness ropes to shake. The other man was yelling, "Whoa, Whoa. Horsie, Whoa."

"The brakes, the brakes!" yelled Father Tailor, remembering what he had heard about automobiles from America. "Hold the brakes."

Father Tailor saw one man bend down inside the car. Suddenly the awful thing came to a halt with loud screech.

The place of merriment was now the scene of a battle field, after the war. Lucille, the young nurse, tore her scarf off to make bandages. Branches of trees were torn down to make splints for broken legs and arms. Moans and groans of the wounded had replaced the joyful cries of "Hoop" and "London Bridge." In the middle of the disaster Mr. Chatterton, the richest man in Nevis, stood with his head in his hands, in his grief forgetting to speak properly:

"A did tink the Ford woulda stop when it see the children and them. A did tink it woulda stop. Me horse always stop. All I have to do is hold the harness and say 'Whoa'."

Lucille listened to the terrified man as her deft fingers tied knots to stop bleeding. Then she remembered the commitment she had made to Darryl moments before the disaster. Yes. She loved him. Yes. One day they would be married. She would ride to the church in Father Tailor's horse and buggy, all cleaned and beautiful for the occasion. Darryl could scrub down the horse the day before, so that it smelled and looked good. Best of all, Lucille was going to her wedding in a carriage pulled by a horse that KNEW when to stop.

15.

Not an Easy Decision

As Darryl rode his bicycle home from his teaching job and thought of the letter he had just received, a feeling of exhilaration overcame him. He couldn't believe the offer. Could there have been some mistake? No. He was the only James Adolphus Walwyn in Nevis. And he was the only Walwyn who taught at Charlestown Boys' School where the letter had been delivered.

Yet Darryl, as James was called, shook his head and concentrated as he passed over Bath Bridge, a narrow footpath just a little wider than his bicycle wheels. He needed to concentrate, because the narrow bridge, his sole route over the Bath River, had seen many travelers fall into its warm water. The water was neither deep nor dangerous, but it would be embarrassing to get home covered with the green moss of the river. When the bridge was passed, Darrel knew he was close to home and would have to break the news to 'Cille his wife of six years. He rode slowly, pondering. If he took the offer, he would have to remove his wife and children from their home, the only home they knew, and go to a place he had never even visited—Parson's Village in St. Kitts, to be a headmaster. If he chose not to go, he would pass up an opportunity for a big promotion. Who knew when such an offer would come again to a young male teacher like him?

Darryl walked slowly up to his front door. He could hear the Bath Stream murmuring gently on its way to the seashore. He could hear the waves pounding on the beach a few steps away. He could smell that "Bath River smell"—the scent of moss and sulphur and warm water. From inside the house, he could make out the sound of singing. That must be Amorelle, he thought. That child was always singing. If she kept that up, she would be a musician some day. Darryl smiled at the thought. He too loved music, and was proud that his four-year-old seemed to have inherited that love from him. Darryl could also hear the chatter of his baby, his two-year-old, Annette. That child, whose face mirrored his, seemed to have a special love for this teacher-father of hers. He smiled at the thought that one day, she too, might become a teacher. He had so many plans for these two precious children.

Darryl could not yet enter the house and face his wife with the news. His eyes misted as he remembered the other child, the one who had never cried. The one who was born silent five years ago, and was now buried in the graveyard near the Governor's mansion. How could he go and leave her little grave? Who would plant violets and roses, and who would pull the weeds from the grave of his firstborn?

Darryl slowly dismounted from the bicycle and walked up the front steps. As soon as the door was opened, Darryl's feet were grasped firmly, his bag was taken, and four little arms held this man captive.

"Lucille, I'm home."

He could hardly see his wife's face for the hugs and kisses that greeted his arrival. Coming home was a daily thrill for Darryl—a joy that he anticipated as he taught the sometimes hardheaded boys in Charlestown. Though Darryl had always loved children, he never knew how much he could love them until he had his own two little girls. Life was perfect, Darryl thought. How can I take my wife and little girls from this home? How can I interfere with their happiness?

After Amorelle had sung him a song she had "composed" that day, and after Annette "read" her father a story she had made up, it was time for dinner.

"You are really quiet tonight, Darryl," observed his wife. "Did you have a difficult day at school?"

"No, Dear. Today was fine. But I got a letter from the Education Department, and it is making me worry. I don't know what to do. I might as well tell you now, and the children can hear it too. They want me to be a headmaster..."

"But that's great, dear. That's just the sort of promotion you have been waiting for. I..."

"Wait. You have not heard all of it. They want me to move to St. Kitts to a place called Parson's Village."

"And leave all of your family here in Nevis? And what about the children? They will have to grow up without their cousins. I can't tell Mother Tailor this. She is sick in bed and I don't know how she will manage if I am not there to help her. And Father Tailor loves the children so."

"I have not yet decided, Cille. But one thing I know is that I am not going anywhere without you and the children. Who knows? It may be God's will for us to move away from here."

Seeing the solemn looks on their parents' faces, the children were silent, sensing, as children always can, a change in the barometer of their secure home.

Home for them meant Sunday trips to the bath stream where their mother, with other Charletown mothers, washed clothes in the warm water of the Bath Stream. It meant playing naked with their cousins and other girls in the "ladies" part of the stream and going home with clean bodies and clean clothes, feeling new.

There was no Bath Stream in St. Kitts.

Home meant riding to church, even crossing the Bath Bridge, with their father and mother on Lillie, the bicycle. No one in Nevis could understand how Darryl, his wife and his TWO children rode on that bike, especially over that narrow, dangerous bridge. That was home.

There was no narrow Bath Bridge in St. Kitts.

Home meant family—Uncle Frank and Dickie, Auntie Marion and Jamesie, Aunt Adina and Mr. Brown, in Bath Village.

Home was Auntie Olive and Brother John in Mannings; it was Aunt Ursula and Son in Charlestown.

Home meant playing "Hoop" and "Ring Around the Roses" on moonlight nights with Iola and Brontie and Carol and all of their other cousins down by Teacher Dina's school.

In their little hearts the children knew what home meant, and they sensed a threat to the security they knew. So they cried as they felt the threat as only children can.

Darkness had fallen as the family grieved, and Darryl got up slowly, taking the baby in his arms. He wanted to take his customary walk after dinner. Tonight his walk took him down to the sea shore.

As Darryl walked along the beach, deep in thought, he looked at the horizon and could see the lights of St. Kitts in the distance. St. Kitts did not look so far away after all, he thought. He could always come back for Christmas, for summer, and for weekends.

And in St. Kitts he would have the opportunity to make a better life for his wife and girls. Perhaps Amorelle could even get music lessons when she was old enough. Perhaps both girls could get into Miss Langley's Girls School one day.

Inside the house Lucille was thinking: perhaps going to St. Kitts had some merit. She was a qualified nurse, a midwife. She could get a job anywhere. It would definitely be better for Darryl to get that job in St. Kitts. What an opportunity for a young man! She would get someone to look after Mother Tailor, her adopted mother, in Nevis. She could visit her family in Nevis on weekends and at Christmas sometimes. How could she ever stand in the way of an opportunity like this for her husband?

As Darryl came in with the now sleeping child, he approached his wife and searched her face for an answer as she searched his. But not a word was spoken as they put little nighties on the two sleeping children, turned down the wick of the lamp, and prepared to go to bed themselves. Then the words came, as husband and wife lay side by side on the narrow bed— words that revealed the opportunities of St. Kitts—the music, the schools; the problem of leaving home, the challenge of starting over. But as they held each other and tears mixed with laughter, Lucille and Darryl realized that Kitts would never be Nevis, but it would not be so bad after all.

16.

Nine Lives

Any decent cat would have been seriously jealous of Sunny. For while that cat could boast nine lives, it seemed that Sunny had been blessed with at least twice that number. He had crashed a car on Frigate Bay Road and had walked away without even a bump on his head. The car could not be repaired.

The motorcycle was his next catastrophe. It was a powerful Oxford, with side panels and polished, chrome fittings. It had overturned with him near Conaree Beach one rainy night. The motorcycle had slammed into a house near Bay Road, destroying door, sofa, a few windows, and a new stereo set. The vehicle stopped before it reached the bedroom, or there would have been at least one death. But where was Sunny? He had dusted off his clothes and collected money from the insurance company to buy a new motorcycle.

Things got so bad that insurance companies would not insure Sunny. He was not just a bad risk. He was a liability. Only the daring would go out with him. For usually, he would walk home, alone, at all hours, after the ambulance had picked up his companions.

So it was with some fear that people saw Sunny down by the pier in Basseterre on August 1. August Monday was just two days away and the pier was "jammed" full of people. Tired commuters from Nevis were there, anxious to rejoin their families and spend an extra day at home in Gingerland or Mannings. Nevis merchants with huge baskets on their heads had already bought shoes and treats for their children. Many were sitting on the pier in the waning light, hoping to be home before it was too dark.

The pier was full of tourists from the U.S. and from England—some of them nationals returning home, having given up their passports, but not the love for their hometown.

Children were going to spend time with relatives in Nevis. There they stood with little suitcases and big smiles. August Monday in Nevis would be a lot of fun.

And in the midst of the crowd on the pier, stood Sunny—tall, brown, and handsome. He was going to Nevis for August Monday. But he traveled like a scout—only a little bag over his shoulders.

The captain scanned the crowd on the pier. There was a look of consternation on his face. So many people. So much luggage. How was the boat going to carry all of that stuff? The maximum capacity was 200 people, and already a rough count showed him that there seemed to be at least 300 people waiting. He had had an overload before. This was not the first time. Maybe he could do it again. This was the last trip to Nevis before the August Monday celebration. How could he disappoint so many people? And which ones could he deny passage to? He would just have to try to make it.

The Christina creaked at the side of the pier that day as passengers boarded. The deck was full of the steel-band lovers who already had instruments ready for an on-board party. The tired were in the hold of the ship, glad to have seats after working hard all day. In the captain's cabin, rum had already begun to flow and card games had been produced. It was going to be some trip.

Sunny had joined the latter group. He would divide his time between the steel-band players and the rum and card gang down below.

With a loud blast of the horn the ship heaved anchor and settled itself for the hour-long trip. The ship appeared to groan like a market woman whose bags are just a bit too heavy. It cut a blue swath on the afternoon waters and turned its prow to Nevis.

Captain Ansel, still full of misgivings, looked around him. The crowd seemed to be 400, or was it his imagination? People seemed to be everywhere. Bags and boxes crowded every path. He hoped the next hour would pass quickly.

"OK Cap?" he heard at his elbow. It was Sunny, all smiles.

"Yea, Man. A lot o' people, but we going try. The Ol'girl have more than she can handle today, and I leave people on the pier, but is the holiday coming up. You know how that is."

The captain smiled wearily at Sunny. The hour would soon be up.

The Christina ploughed through the water heavily. The steel band was deafening, and, in spite of the roll of the ship, people were dancing wildly. The noise from the card game in the hold below competed with the steel band. In spite of the crowd and the noise, tired commuters slept.

Booby Island and the Channel between St. Kitts and Nevis appeared to the left of the Christina. The Channel was always the worst part of the trip, and Captain Ansel hoped that the Channel crossing would not be too bad today. The ship rocked to the right and then to the left. This was the Channel, passengers realized. The sleepers did not even wake up. The steel band was not disturbed. Some dancers moved a little more drunkenly, but certainly did not stop the dance.

The Christina seemed to be taking the challenge of the Channel all right, when suddenly she keeled over, spilling 400 people into the Caribbean Sea—the worst disaster by sea that the little islands had ever known.

The blue waves suddenly took on a different appearance. There were baskets floating besides steel band drums, old hats and jaunty carnival hats floated side by side on the dark water. It somehow looked like a deadly carnival. Shrill screams competed with muffled cries as men, women and children struggled to keep afloat. Many held on to the sides of the boat, sides slippery from the sea moss and encrusted with sea creatures. Some in the hold of the ship were trapped. Some people held on to the proverbial straw, only to see it sink, with them, beneath the waters. With no help in sight, the brave began to swim. Hours later, rescuers came upon the grim scene, the graveyard for hundreds of travelers.

For several days, sickened rescuers picked up bodies: of children going on vacation to Nevis, a whole family that had come from England for a vacation, commuters who would never take the trip to work again. Some were bloated beyond recognition and, never identified, were buried beside fellow travelers in graves marked by rows of simple crosses. Some people simply disappeared. Hundreds of people perished that day, and the Christina still sits at the bottom of the sea floor.

Remarkably, over 100 people survived. With his nine lives, Sonny swam, fully dressed, for three hours. Sunny washed at Pinney's Beach that evening—cramped, sore, and parched, but very much alive.

17.

The Cockroach

That Friday morning, Miss Sadie got up, aware that there was only a piece of saltfish in the house. Nothing else. All her eddoes, her sweet potatoes and salt beef were done—finished when she cooked "man soup" for that man the day before. He had eaten her soup, sprawled out on the settee, and gone to sleep. In the morning he was gone, had crawled out like a cockroach, Miss Sadie thought with tears in her eyes. As Boysie ate hungrily, Sadie had noticed the large eyes of her hungry children. But she had gambled. I feed him today, he gives me money for the children tomorrow. She had gambled and she had lost. Today the children's hungry eyes would look into hers again, and the three boys would suck their thumbs until they turned color, and she would have to depend on the generosity of her neighbors to make it through another day.

Miss Sadie thought of other days. She remembered the days when Boysie, the children's father, a handsome Montserratan with false teeth, had won her with stories of his time at sea:

"Girl, the sea turn up so bad when we leave Curacao going to Aruba. I thought we was dead meat. The waves and them crashing over the boat, and people bailing, bailing. But as fast as they bail, water come back in. Me Crosses. Then the storm pass, and the next day the sea so calm, like somebody throw oil on it."

"And, Girl, you never see so much flying fish as that morning near Barbados. I thought I was seeing things. The flying fish leaping out of the water like they having high jump contest."

Sadie had laughed. She had never left St. Kitts. Had hardly been out of Basseterre. The stories of this knowledgeable man held her captive. She was sure that he was the smartest man in the world. She fell hopelessly in love, although neighbors warned her:

"Watch out for them sea man and them. They have a woman in every port and pickney besides. Them look sweet and talk fine but don't trust them. Mark what me say."

Those neighbors were talking to the wind. It was almost as if they were telling Sadie, "Morning Peter" with Sadie giving the fabled, foolish reply in St. Kitts, "Cabbage, Ma'am."

Sadie was in love and did not know what hit her until she noticed the morning sickness. She named the child Peter, after the famous fisherman in the Bible. In quick succession James and John similarly named, joined little Peter. Like their mother, they enjoyed hearing the stories their handsome sailor father told. They loved the toys he brought for them.

"I buy this in Aruba," he told Peter, giving him a Dutch game. The boy smiled proudly. No other boy in his class would have anything like that. What a father! Peter had even learned a few words in Papiamente, the Dutch Creole dialect, from his seafaring Dad.

But still the neighbors told Sadie,

"Girl, when you looks gone, Boysie gone too. Don't get any grey hair, your hear me? Stay young and pretty, or you going end up crying, I tell you. Stay pretty."

Sadie had been Boysie's common-law-wife for six years now. She saw him every month or so. The loud blast of the merchant boat would blow, and soon there would be the familiar sounds of his coming. Sadie would hear the scraping of leather shoes on the step, and someone clearing his throat. She and the boys would compete to see who could greet him first. Before Boysie left again, he would leave money—enough for Sadie to live like a queen until he returned. Her home took on the look of a Kittitian palace. No one around had the trinkets, the table cloths, the dishes that she had.

Sadie was still pretty six years later when she noticed that sometimes she would not see Boysie for two months at a time. Then for four months. Soon it was a six-month break. She looked into the mirror and saw no change except for the thin line of grey at her temples. Her cheeks were sagging just a little. Perhaps she had not slept so well the last few nights, Sadie tried to fool herself. She knew her Boysie. Those neighbors only wanted to get into people's business. She wouldn't even bother to try to explain to them. And they were jealous. That's it. Jealous of her and Boysie. They would not understand.

But Sadie realized that she was having a harder time keeping food in the house and clothes on the backs of the growing boys. The money Boysie had brought the last time had finished long ago, and the boys had begun sucking their thumbs again. Sometimes in the night, Sadie would hear the loud sucking. The sound would wake her up. How could she get cornmeal for the boys to make some "corn pap"? Thick, warm corn meal "pap" would keep them full for a few hours at least. And where was Boysie? Shame kept Sadie from meeting her neighbors' eyes. She remembered their words:

"Girl when you looks gone..."

"Them sailormen does have a woman in every..."

"No! Stop it!" Sadie screamed inside. "He still loves me. Perhaps there has been an accident at sea. Perhaps Boysie is not well."

So when Boysie had showed up on her doorstep the next morning in his handsome "foreign" clothes and shoes, when she heard his stories of Panama and Curaco, Sadie forgot all her worries. Boysie had given the boys toys, and surely he would give Sadie money before he left. She opened her windows wide for her neighbors to hear Boysie's voice. She used all her eddoes and salt beef to make him a man soup that could be smelled in every house for miles around. Boysie had eaten, had fallen asleep, and had crept away like a cockroach in the night as the hungry boys sucked their fingers.

When Sadie stopped crying the next day, she realized it was now a matter of survival, for herself and the boys, She must be strong for those boys. She must get food for them. She had no one to depend on. Boysie was gone, and if he came back like a cockroach, he would get what every cockroach that showed its head got. She would be waiting for him.

In her anger, Sadie became creative. She began to entertain her neighbors, even if it was only with "bebbrige," a drink made of sugar and water. Neighbors would get an earful of what she planned to do to that cockroach and how he would regret ever showing up in Basseterre.

But Sadie was surviving. Every neighbor who came by brought a pound of rice or a cup of cornmeal. "For de children," they would say. Neighbors who went fishing would bring a few jackfish or a pound of fresh, sweet balahoo for Sadie. Some would drop by to talk and leave a few sweet potatoes, a few heads of chives and thyme, or a few onions. Sadie herself planted ground provisions. She learned how to grow eddoes and yellow yam.

Thus the boys ate everyday. Not sumptuously, but they had "nuff food." Fruit was plentiful, for the boys often filled up on sour ginips, guavas, and mangoes. The boys especially loved the sweet rosy cheeked mangoes from a tree behind the house. Peter knew how to use the stick picker to pull down the ripe mangoes instead of waiting for them to fall. Breadfruit was plentiful, and Sadie learned how to make breadfruit porridge for breakfast, and then roast the rest of the breadfruit with mackerel for lunch. The boys loved the filling meal, washed down with bebbrige, sugar and water.

And the growing boys were never naked. Someone was always bringing a clean, darned pair of pants for one of the boys, or a polished, though worn pair of shoes. That's how people in St. Kitts live, Sadie realized thankfully. She and the boys would neither starve nor go naked.

It had been three years since Boysie's last visit. Three years of watching the merchant ships arrive and leave without the sight of that handsome face. Each time a merchant boat's horn sounded, Sadie's heart would beat anxiously, beat with a hope that perhaps this time he was coming, perhaps there had been an accident, perhaps.... But after each disappointment the anxiety grew less, replaced with a growing hatred for the man who would leave his family without even goodbye. Sadie imagined him visiting other ports and telling some other woman his stories and his lies. She imagined babies looking like Peter, James and John on some island, and she grew angry. A person can train himself or herself not to hear certain sounds, and so to Sadie's ears, there were no merchant ships, no Boysie.

Peter, James, and John were putting on size, however, eating food through their neighbors' generosity and wearing clean hand-me-down clothes. John still sucked his finger, but more for comfort than from hunger. Peter and James had long ago stopped. But Peter, now fourteen years old, stood taller than his mother. He smiled just like his father and had his father's charm. One day Peter told his mother something that he had been contemplating for a long time; he made the mistake to tell his mother that he wanted to become a seaman like his father.

"I want to go see places, Mom, " he said one evening. "Like Pa. I want to go to Panama and Aruba and all them places."

"Over my dead body," was his mother's reply. "And don't you ever mention that man's name in this house again. If it was not for them neighbors you and you brothers would be dead long ago. That man turn off and don't even remember... That man is a ... Let me hold me tongue. You want to be a seaman? You want to be a seaman? Dem seamen does have a woman in every port and picney too. Is that what you want?"

Sadie's tirade was interrupted by a familiar knock at the door. Leather shoes were scraping the steps as they prepared to enter the house. Sadie heard all and covered the dough she was kneading to make dumplings. In the worn apron she wiped trembling hands. Then and only then did she grab the broomstick from behind the door.

There was only one way to deal with a cockroach.

18.

"We Won't Reach": a Honeymoon in St. Kitts

Everyone who has a choice should honeymoon in St.Kitts as we did. But go there with this warning: avoid Taxi Number 646. When the travel agent recommended Basseterre, St. Kitts, we were not so sure we wanted to go. Did they have hotels?

The finest, we were told. Pictures of Sea View, a hotel near the sea, captivated us. The travel agent assured us that this place was a favorite of honeymooners, and that she had spent a week there herself.

Assured of four-star treatment, we had to get accustomed to pronouncing the name of the place, which we thought was Bass E Terre. We were told that Basseterre or Bass E terre (whichever) was the capital of St. Kitts/ St. Christopher. We got mixed up—St. Christopher? St. Kitts? The second name was a shortened form of the first, we heard. That explanation didn't seem to make much sense, but historic Brimstone Hill and Frigate Bay sounded appealing. So we bought our tickets, got married, and changed planes in Antigua for our trip to St. Kitts.

After we had cleared customs in Basseterre/Bass E terre/BassTerre, we stepped outside waiting for the taxi which our four-star hotel had promised to send. At first we did not mind waiting in the warm December afternoon, remembering faintly the chilly Baltimore weather we had left.

On a honeymoon, one does not look at the clock. But after half an hour and many polite "No Thank You's " to solicitous taxi drivers, we decided to try to find Sea View ourselves. Leaving Baltimore, Maryland, we had to be cautious, however. Suppose a taxi driver robbed us or killed us. Suppose he stole our passports?

We finally said "OK" to an older, serious-looking driver. At his age, if he were going to be a killer, he would have been in jail a long time ago, we thought. We were impressed with his courtesy. His British manners. His polite "Yes Ma'am" "No Ma'am." His pleasant smile. However, other drivers standing around looked a bit concerned, and we felt guilty. But we were not to blame. It was just our luck to pick the best. The other drivers would just have to understand that.

Trying not to glance back at their disappointed faces, we approached our "ride." The car was clean— spotless— actually, inside and outside, but it had an air of antiquity. Feelings of regret began to surface and we hoped they did not show. We had to step up to the seats. We could not close the door. It had to be closed for us by our smiling driver. He slammed it with an expert click. With heads almost hitting the roof of the Model C, we jerked forward as he slid the car into first gear. In Baltimore, the pain we felt in our necks would have been called whiplash, but we were afraid to complain. Mr. Polite was still a taxi-driver. Suppose he took our wallets and left us at the side of the road? Holding each other more for security than for love, we peered out of the windows.

This was our first full realization that we were in trouble. We seemed to be standing still, though the car was supposed to be moving. Yes, we wanted to see the scenery of Basseterre, but sitting still in an uncomfortable car was not the way to do it. We looked at the panel of the car to see if the ignition was really on, and noticed that the speedometer read 15 miles per hour. Fifteen! A baby could walk fifteen miles an hour. My new husband had stopped smiling.

"Excuse me, Sir. Could you step on it? We have a dinner reservation for six o'clock."

"We will reach," was his taciturn reply, a reply that we would get accustomed to as the day wore on.

"Can we stop somewhere to call and confirm our dinner reservations?"

He turned to us and smiled,

"We will reach."

One does not worry on a honeymoon, so worry was turning ours into something bizarre. Right and left of us, a few cars were passing our driver. Ten taxi drivers at the airport, and we had to end up with this turtle and his Model F. Several drivers honked their horns in exasperation, we thought, but soon we realized that honking was the St. Christopher way of saying hello. These were quite friendly and fast-driving people, all except our driver.

By 5:45 we realized that unless Sea View was at the next corner, we would definitely be late. Well, perhaps we could find a McDonalds or forget food. One does not have to eat on a honeymoon. We could live on love, if we could ever get out of this car.

Why hadn't we thought of renting a car at the airport? Why hadn't we ....

"You are now passing Market Street."

Nice of you to tell us. But where's Sea View? Does one hijack a taxi?

As if the driver had read out minds he murmured.

"We not long passed the local jail. Kittitian jailers are known for taking things literally. When a person has five years hard time, it means five years HARD TIME."

Hard time? We were doing hard time in this ancient buggy. We looked at each other and eyes spoke what lips feared to utter.

"Hard time means that you go in chains to do jobs like cleaning the cemetery which is a showplace in St. Kitts. Hard time means going up to the schools with a cutlass to cut down the grass and to pick up the garbage. Hard time means...".

O, shut up and drive. Our eyes spoke these words though our faces, fearing attack, forced tired smiles. "Are we almost there?" It was 6:30.

"We will reach. To your left is Greenlands, a new housing development. If you want to settle in St. Kitts, here would be a good place..."

O, be quiet. We want to reach our beds. Perhaps you only have to crawl into your shell, but we have paid for a honeymoon suite. Paid good money, too.

"for you to buy a house or a piece of land..."

By now the sun was setting with a glorious gold and red. St. Kitts was a beautiful place, but would we have to see it only through the dull window of this First Edition Ford?

"Here is our lovely cemetery. The governor's mansion is beyond it. Tourists make visits to both places. This cemetery is said to be one of the finest in the Caribbean."

It would be nice if we could see more than silhouettes of the graves, Mister Turtle. Perhaps if you had been driving at even 20 miles an hour, night would not have met us on this ghastly trip. My husband's eyes met mine. But politely he asked,

"What is the speed limit here?"

"We will..."

Reach. Yes. We knew, even if it meant next week. Would the hotel give us a refund if we got there seven days late? Could we sue Sea View for not having a taxi sent to us as planned?

"We are now entering The Village."

What village? The only village we want to see is the one marked Sea View.

A look of desperation had appeared on my new husband's face. *Why did we not stay in New York? At least we could have taken the subway to the Biliot Hotel. The wedding had been so special. Where had we gone wrong? Perhaps we should not have gotten married.* I heard a voice I had never heard before.

"I must use the bathroom, Sir."

"We are almost there. You can find one in the lobby. Hope you enjoyed the drive."

In the darkness we had not seen Sea View loom before us. As we climbed stiffly down the steps of Ford I, we looked around us. The hotel overlooked a perfectly shaped half-moon bay. A new moon was shining, stars were out, and a million lights shone on the quiet sea before us. Perhaps we could salvage the honeymoon after all.

"That will be ten dollars."

We paid the fare, grabbed our luggage, and checked into our honeymoon suite. Complimentary glasses of Pina Colada and cool champagne welcomed us. On a side table we chose from an assortment of tropical fruits that smelled even more delicious than they looked. A note invited us to sample orange-colored Julie mangoes and mamsiport. Though we had missed the meal, the sandwiches and fruit satisfied us until breakfast time.

All too soon a week had gone by. We had tried in vain to imitate the sing-song lilt of the Kittitians. But we had learned to eat sweet Conkee wrapped in savory banana leaves, to drink coconut water from freshly cut coconuts, and to eat the sour ginips which were in season. We loved swimming at Frigate Bay. We had bought tee shirts and conch shells to take back to Baltimore. We had made many friends with so many Kittitians. All memories of the disastrous ride from the airport had faded. It was time to return to Baltimore to begin our new life together.

Bags packed, we waited at the checkout desk, saying goodbye to the staff we had come to know by name. A last trip to the beach had given us only half an hour to check in at the airport. With sand in our hair and shoes, we did not mind.

Suddenly I saw fear in my husband's eyes. He was looking at the door. I was afraid to follow his glance. I had not seen that look on his face since that taxi ride a week ago. Then I heard a voice that drew all the joy of the vacation into a tiny ball and rammed it down my parched throat. At the door stood a small, smiling man saying three words:

"We will reach."

19.

Only a Piece of Cane

Sammy should have known that today was not his day from morning. When he went to the standpipe to" head" water, the bucket had splashed water all over him. He was down, soaking wet before the barrel outside his house was full. If he did not fill the barrel, he could not go to school. His mother would not let him go until he had done the job. She needed the water to wash the Arthurtons' clothes by hand as she did each week in the big copper tank behind the house. The money she got from that job was not much, but it put sardines and stale bread on the table for herself, Sammy and his five small sisters.

When Sammy looked up Thibou Avenue, he did not see ManMan or Roy. It must be late, or they would not have left for school without him. Sammy began to worry. If he were late for school again, Head Teacher Moore would beat him in front of everybody at Basseterre Boys' School. Sammy changed his shirt and hurriedly looked for his other pair of pants, but remembered that the hole in the seat of the pants had burst open again, and his underwear would show.

The boy knew instinctively that he should not go to school today, at least not until his good pants were dry, but his mother would hear nothing about his staying at home.

"Boy, you drunk? What you think dey mek school for? You going even if you reach school one o'clock dis afternoon. You going learn to read and write. You going to Grammar School too. I want to see you come out better than me. I have it too hard. Me fingers and dem old before they time from washing other people clothes. I want something better for me children."

"But Mama..."

"Don't but me nothing. I don't want to hear it. You want to be a good-for-nothing like you father? Is that what you want? I will show you how to be a vagabond. Just pass the leather. I will show you."

Against such argument, Sammy made a speedy retreat down the rickety steps without shoes, books, and pencils—almost without his wet pants.

Sammy knew his mother had a point. For all his life he had heard his mother tell about his vagabond father, about his drinking, his cursing, his thieving, his women. His mother watched Sammy like a mother hen, ready to pluck out any trace of his "fader" that she could spot. His father could not read. Sammy would go to school even if it meant that he was so late he got a severe beating for it. She realized he was tardy because he was helping her at home, but she could not spare him from there either. The only boy, and the first child, he was her right hand, left hand and sometimes her feet.

As Sammy rushed around the corner of Thibou Avenue, the nine o'clock bell was ringing. Head Teacher Moore would be beating latecomers now. Sammy's back had felt that strap twice already this week. How could he go to school? His feet dragged but went steadily in the direction of Basseterre Boys' School.

Sammy passed other boys who were not going to school. There was Bobo, the slow boy. People said he was "cracked" in his head from an accident at birth. He wore a permanent smile on his face even when the other boys were beating him up, as if he did not understand or did not care. Bobo was playing ball with Nathan, the school bully. Everyone was glad when Nathan did not go to school, even Nathan's mother. Every time he went to school, she would have to go to the police station on Cayon Street to bring him back home, and he would be spattered with someone's blood, again.

But Sammy was not like those boys. He loved to study, especially geography, to see all those countries like Australia and France. The United States fascinated him, and he would dream that he went to sleep and woke up in the Rocky Mountain Range, or on the Great Plains. They looked so small on the map. Sammy would put his hand on a spot and say "here," meaning that he had found a place to put his three-bedroom house like those at Taylor's Range. His house would have glass windows and a real flush toilet. Sammy would flush that toilet loudly so all his neighbors could know that he had one.

Sammy would often dream like this in class, and get beaten on his knuckles by Teacher David when he couldn't answer a question. Sammy would not mind the pain of the beating. What he hated was that he would have to start dreaming all over again after the beating.

"Sammy, come play cricket with us. We need a spin bowler." This was Nathan's invitation.

"You all making joke. I got to go school. I don't want no trouble."

"But you done in trouble. Look how late it is. You may as well stay with us. You want us go hunt ground lizard? grasshopper? You want us go bother those girls in Miss Sebastian School?

"No. You all go ahead. I going to school."

Sammy ran without looking back. He wasn't sure he was going to school because he was so late, but he did not want to be seen with either Nathan or Bobo.

When he reached the school, Head Teacher Moore was at the door with the leather belt in his hand. The belt was long and brown—cowhide. Sammy was sure that the headmaster had sent to England for the longest, thickest belt and had it delivered to the Basseterre Boys' School. Grown men in Basseterre spoke with dread about that belt and looked closely at Teacher Moore's hand even when they saw him ten years after they had left school. Yes, sir. That belt had a reputation all its own.

Sammy tried going round to the back of the school, but Head Teacher Moore saw him and called him.

"Samuel Hart, what you think you are doing coming in here at this hour? The reading lesson is over and Arithmetic is about to start. You are late, late. I am not going to stand here and see you become a reprobate like your father. No, Sir. Furthermore, what are you thinking of doing coming in here wet and dirty? Don't you have any pride in yourself? Do you think you going to land in jail like your worthless father? Come here. Come here."

"But Teacher Moore, I..."

"I don't want to hear any excuse, boy. Worthlessness is what has you coming in at this time. Come here, I say."

Sammy could feel the recent lashes still stinging under his thin shirt. The welts would surely burst open if he got any more licks.

He stepped forward one step.

Two steps

Three steps.

The headmaster was flexing the brown monster that curled and seemed to lick its lips in anticipation.

Four steps, and the first blow.

"You will not be like your worthless, LASH, father, not if I have to beat you till every hair on your back comes off, LASH. Not if I have to beat you within an inch of your life. LASH"

Sammy felt something wet on his back and knew it was not perspiration. He felt his shirt stick to his back. He realized he smelled blood, his own blood.

A muffled cry. A full-fledged scream. Sammy had had enough. He turned, and ran full speed from the headmaster's destructive blows. He did not stop running, taking all kinds of back alleys, until he was in Shadwell Estate.

The boy could see the tall fields of ripe cane and hear the swish as the canecutters leveled the fields with their expert machetes. If only he was old enough to cut cane, then he could make some money and help his mother. Then she would not have to work so hard. Maybe she wouldn't be so cross all of the time. Maybe she would not be telling Sammy about his father all of the time as she was doing.

Sammy now realized that he had not eaten all day. He had rushed out of his home without his bush tea and his penny bread. His back hurt from the beating and from the shirt stuck to the raw flesh. His stomach hurt from hunger, but most of all, something deep inside hurt from poverty, and shame, and anger at all of it.

The ground near Sammy shook as the locomotive full of cane approached on its way to the sugar factory. Without even thinking about it, Sammy leapt aboard, holding on to the stalks of cane that were leaning over the side. He was too weak from hunger and fatigue to break the cane in the fields, and he would get into trouble if he were caught, anyway. Jumping on the moving locomotive was not something he had planned to do, but he was hungry, and there was all of that freshly cut cane inside.

The locomotive was picking up speed, now, and gave out a long hoot as it passed near Dr. Lake's house on its way to the Sugar Factory. The speed of the train created a cool breeze that was refreshing to the child's bleeding back. If only he could get a good hold of one long stalk of cane and pull it out! He tried, and after some difficulty got a long, clear stalk of cane in his hands. His teeth grasping one end and his hand the other, Sammy peeled the cane and enjoyed the sweet, sweet juice that ran down his face, his hands, and his shirt. Yes! This was better than staying in school and getting beaten by the headmaster. Sammy pulled out one cane after another until he actually felt full.

There in his bed of cane Sammy began to dream that he was in the Rocky Mountains and had begun to build his three-bedroom house with the glass windows. The house was big, with rooms for his mother and sisters. Sammy had just installed the flush toilet when he looked up and realized that the flush he heard was the sound of the sugar stalks being poured into a crushing bin. His frightened gaze looked into metal jaws that opened, grasped cane and boy, but kept rolling. Sammy's muffled screams caught the operator's attention. Rushing to stop the inevitable, he cried:

"Look, mearm, is a boy in there. I can't even get this thing to stop. HELP ME SOMEBODY. I just imagine I hear something. Me crosses. Is a boy. Look he foot. Let me see if he still alive. SOMEBODY, HELP!"

But the damage was done.

When the huge machine shuddered to a stop, frantic cane handlers puked as they pulled out the mangled remains. Machines intended for separating the cane stalks from the thrash that covered them had ripped the child as if he were a rag doll. Bones and intestines lay exposed on the teeth of the monstrous thing like pieces of some worthless toy.

There was a funeral at the Moravian church the next day. A child's funeral. In the front pew sat five little girls who stared at the plain pine coffin. Sammy's mother was there in her only black dress, her eyes swollen from crying all night.

"I did send him to school. I tell him not to become like his no-good father. And now, look what he do. I did only send him to school. He harden. He wouldn't listen to his poor old mother. He mean he going turn out like he good-for-nothing father."

Head Teacher Moore gave the obituary:

"Sammy was a good boy. I wish I could have encouraged him to like school. I wish I could have done more to steer Sammy in the right direction...."

In the distance, a sugar cane locomotive rumbled by, blowing a shrill blast as it passed Dr. Lake's house on its way to the Sugar Factory with its load of cane. And in the schoolyard, Bobo the slow boy, the one with the "cracked" head smiled, and bowled the ball to Nathan.

20.

Dried Tamarinds

The rainy months had passed, and the dry spell in April brought a familiar sound—the rattle of dried fruit on the tamarind trees at Frigate Bay just outside of Basseterre. The old trees seemed to have been there forever, always looking the same—gnarled branches that seemed to have always been old, with clusters of blossoms that turned "floury" in February, that turned dry in April. Those old trees knew the loneliness of off-season, when no one except lizards and ants cared for the company of the old trees that were now bare of fruit. They knew the comfort of wind and rain and the closeness of hot sun on those lonely days. But those trees knew companionship—the sound of running feet, the shrieks of delight at the dry feel of the tamarind shells, and the grasping hands that filled bag after bag with dried tamarinds. Those trees knew the smacking sounds of tongues and lips attacking the sometimes bitter, sometimes sweet fruit.

Doris walked home slowly, passing the Square, Bakers' Corner, and the truck stop. Civil servants were hurrying home, crossing the street quickly to escape the speeding traffic. Tired domestics dragged themselves home to another round of sweeping, dusting, washing. Doris felt annoyed at their eagerness. Since the separation she hated going home—hated seeing his picture on the wall, hated remembering where he used to sit, remembering his smell, remembering his last angry exit and his demand for time and space.

Today was their anniversary. Doris passed her hand over her eyes and was surprised to feel her hand trembling. She must have a few minutes to "ketch" herself. The children must not see her this way. Just a few more minutes.

At Frigate Bay, little waves splashed gently on the evening shore. A blood-red sun was setting in the west, casting long bony shadows on the warm water. The tired tamarind trees felt the call of evening and sighed. Tiny leaves rustled and sun-dried tamarinds shook in their shells.

At the corner of Lozack Road, a mangy almost hairless dog wagged its tail at Doris. Five o'clock. Where was the scrap of bread she usually had for him? Today Doris's eyes could see nothing but the letter that was burned into her mind— a letter from a lawyer that began, "Divorce proceedings have begun on behalf of my client..."
No! Not Divorce! Tell Basil to come home. It is all a big mistake. He was just angry that I was vexed. Tell him we'll work it out. Doris's eyes screamed these words, but only a frightened whimper escaped her lips. His long tail lowering, mangy dog slunk away. No greeting, no bread, no smile today.
Her children would be all right if she was late getting home, Doris knew. They would think she had stopped at Mr. Amory's Bakery and had met some friends. But she actually gave the children only a fleeting thought. The anger, hurt, madness she felt were like little breezes, destructive little breezes, harmless by themselves, but combined became a hurricane brewing inside the Gulf Coast of Doris's head.

Waves splashed up near the foot of the tamarind tree, the old, gnarled tree, with its marked trunk. On its left side lovers' initials and a crooked heart were carved. Were they SR and GT? It was hard to tell after all those years. The old tree shook its little leaves and its bitter, dried tamarinds rattled against each other. It was still early in the tamarind season. Two weeks ago, one group of pickers had already found the tamarinds in their half-ripe "floury" stage. These pickers would be back in a couple of days. The old tree would be only too happy to give up its acid fruit. But today was Wednesday, not even half-day. No company today. Perhaps tomorrow.

Doris walked past the street she had called home for twelve years. She had to have time to think, and by herself, not with Solomon pestering her to let him play cricket at Warner Park, or with Monica practicing her scales for the millionth time. Not today. Her mind spun like a tape rewinding:

What a wedding it had been at the Anglican Church twelve years ago! So much goat water, such sweet souse, blood pudding for days. Doris had tried to stifle the misgivings she still felt, the quiet voice of her father saying over and over again, " A don't trust dem Soho boys. I hear too much bad ting 'bout dem. Watch you case, girl. Watch you case." She had tried to forget the promise she had made to herself to never marry a boy from Basseterre. They were too "fresh," liked too many girls, and had trouble keeping promises.

In the excitement of the Anglican wedding, however, forgetting such worries was not hard. Father Charles had even made jokes as he had the couple repeat, "For better, for worse," not, as the minister had pointed out to the amused crowd, "for better, for better." Doris knew that quite a few girls in Basseterre had watched her with crossed eyes for months after the wedding. She had married their man. And of course, everyone looked at her stomach even during the ceremony. It was common knowledge that a Basseterre boy did not marry any woman unless she was pregnant, if he married her at all. But Doris was not pregnant, and did not have Solomon, her firstborn, until two years after the wedding, a fact that her neighbors talked about in awed tones for years. Today she should be celebrating twelve years of married life, but now, she must face the world and say that it was all a big mistake—the wedding dress, the souse, the children—a mistake that must be thrown out, like a pot of lumpy corn porridge.

No! Let the sun go down and never rise again before she could even begin to accept the idea. Let the moon shine darkly if the wedding day was an error. Let nature scream to the world there had been no April 4, no anniversary, no souse, no dress, no marriage.

A quiet moon shone on the shores of Frigate bay, shone on the water lapping at the sloping shore, shone on the coconut trees like skinny, overgrown boys in short pants chatting at the street corner. The moon shone on the old tamarind tree standing near the shore, the oldest tree of them all. Floury tamarinds, having baked in the April sun, were now dry. In the calm wind, the tamarind shells rubbed each other in a soft, rasping monotone, like eggshells in a garbage bag. They would not have much time together. Any day now a horde of tamarind pickers would arrive and separate them forever from each other—from themselves.

No! The sun must be lying. This was April 4, the twelfth anniversary! But of what? Of happiness, mostly. Every marriage had its troublesome spots, but those were to be expected. Like a sailor about to go down for the last time, Doris could only remember the good times, like the parties that he liked to have—parties for Solomon's christening, Christmas parties that would last until almost New Year's Eve, anniversary parties. It was at the last anniversary party that Basil had met that other woman, or perhaps when the woman came, uninvited, expressly to meet him and set Doris's fairy tale home on fire with gossip. A few days after the party, Basil had begun to leave hints like cattle droppings marking a stink trail:

He had married too soon. He needed space to think. He needed time...

The terrible quarrels started soon after that. Basil found fault with everything Doris said, and everything she did. There was dirt on the floor. A soiled cup was in the sink. Could she not keep the place clean? He did not want ballahoo any more, although he had eaten the fish and licked his fingers clean for eleven years. He had thrown the dish with the rice and fried fish out of the window. Doris could still hear the glass splintering as it hit the guava tree outside. He found fault with her smell, her voice, and her lovemaking. Everything. In two weeks he had moved out of the house.

Doris was now about two miles from her home, the letter still open in her hand, but she was oblivious to the passing traffic, oblivious to the fact that she had passed New Town and was on her way to Frigate Bay, an uninhabited beach. On that walk in the approaching darkness, she relived every day of her married life—her pregnancies, the births of her children, emergency visits to the hospital.

Alone on the deserted road, Doris began to scream, "It ain't fair. Is an abomination. Somebody help me. Tell me what to do. Is my anniversary. Help me, somebody. " Only echoes answered her cries. She passed another mile, and another, and another, her children forgotten, the agonizing pain of the past like a fever, drying up everything inside her, so that she began to feel hollow, as if she had no organs. She had long stopped feeling the pain from her screaming throat, and her feet, now accustomed to the agony from the unaccustomed walk in high heels, had ceased to register any feelings.

It had been some time since Doris had seen a car or a truck. She knew her way only from the moonlight that shone on the dirt road stretching out before her. Her cry had dried up to a moan, and she held her head with both hands, as if it was about to topple off. In her high heels, she stumbled, not realizing how far she had walked.

In the distance waves from Frigate Bay rolled gently to the shore, but Doris could not hear them. A weak moon shone on the water, but Doris's eyes were too swollen to see the lovely sight. A gentle wind blew through the tamarind boughs, but Doris heard not one sound. She could only hear Basil's voice on the phone about six weeks after he had left home,

"It's not going to be forever. I miss you and the children. Let us separate for a few months so I can get my head straight. Believe me, girl, is all for the best—the best—the best—" and like a fool she had believed him. Now the crickets seemed to mock her thoughts –" for worse, for worse, for worse."

At the foot of the tamarind tree, Doris lay down. Without realizing it she had walked seven miles in her pointed high-heeled shoes, but she felt no pain. She had had no dinner, but she felt no hunger. Above her head the tamarinds rattled, a dry rasping sound like leaves on the pavement. A few tamarinds could have made a tasty meal, but Doris did not want tamarinds. She wanted souse, like only Basil could make it. Kittitian men took pride in knowing little about the kitchen, but not Basil. He could cook up a souse that—perhaps it was his souse that had gotten that woman! He had cooked souse for that party when she—. Now the tears began to fall and Doris cried as if the hurricane inside her had passed, leaving only the blinding rain. It must have been near midnight, but she was not sleepy, just drained of all emotion. There must be some way she could stop Basil from going through with the divorce. There must be something, somewhere...

Doris slowly slipped off the belt of her dress.
Then she took the shoes from her swollen feet.
There must be some way.
Some way.
Some way.

The first set of tamarind pickers to Frigate Bay the next morning saw a familiar sight. Waves gently rolled to shore in the brilliant morning sun. Sea birds dipped into the blue water every now and then to catch a fresh snapper for breakfast. Coconut trees stood like scrawny schoolboys in short pants talking at a street corner. And the tamarind trees, the tamarind trees. They were laden. Dried tamarinds rattled in the heated breezes.

But beside the tiny fruit there was another, a larger one, dried not by the gentle April sunshine, but by months of grief. She swung stiff and slow like the tamarinds around her. As the eager pickers reached the old tree, their screams drowned out the sound of the water, the birds, and the dried tamarinds. In the pocket of the dead woman's dress, as she hung from the tree, the trembling children found the letter that began, "Divorce proceedings have begu.."

At the Weslyan funeral later that week, mourners sat stunned in their seats. But two children sat on the front pew looking at the casket that held their mother. They searched the faces of the minister, of the relatives hugging them, the friends sitting near by, and eyes swollen with crying asked the silent question, "Why?"

At Frigate bay, the old tamarind tree bowed its head in grief—all that ripe and bitter fruit untouched on its branches, and the only sweet one, lovely one, was picked the day before. The only sweet one... the only one that was not yet ripe.